Never Enough Time

Never Enough Time

A Practical and Spiritual Guide

Donna Schaper

ROWMAN & LITTLEFIELD
Lanham • Boulder • New York • London

NCR article in chapter 9 originally published in National Catholic Reporter's Eco Catholic blog.

Published by Rowman & Littlefield
An imprint of
The Rowman & Littlefield Publishing Group, Inc.
4501 Forbes Boulevard, Suite 200, Lanham, Maryland 20706
https://rowman.com

Unit A, Whitacre Mews, 26-34 Stannary Street, London SE11 4AB,
United Kingdom

British Library Cataloguing in Publication Information Available

Library of Congress Cataloging-in-Publication Data

Names: Schaper, Donna, author.
Title: Never enough time : a practical and spiritual guide / Donna Schaper.
Description: Lanham : Rowman & Littlefield, [2018] | Includes index.
Identifiers: LCCN 2017046738 (print) | LCCN 2018007124 (ebook) | ISBN
    9781442266391 (Electronic) | ISBN 9781442266384 (cloth : alk. paper)
Subjects: LCSH: Time management--Religious aspects--Christianity. |
    Time--Religious aspects--Christianity. | Simplicity--Religious
    aspects--Christianity.
Classification: LCC BV4598.5 (ebook) | LCC BV4598.5 .S33 2018 (print) | DDC
    650.1/1--dc23
LC record available at https://lccn.loc.gov/2017046738

♾ ™ The paper used in this publication meets the minimum requirements of American National Standard for Information Sciences Permanence of Paper for Printed Library Materials, ANSI/NISO Z39.48-1992.

Printed in the United States of America

Contents

Introduction

So many of us lament that we "just wish we had more time" that the phrase might be our national anthem. We have "bad timing" as an explanation for so many things gone wrong. We ache for "good timing," attributing to it most of the success people find in life. We give our children "time-outs" to manage their behavior. We have really weird relationships with time, even though time is as ordinary as ordinary can be.

Bad timing is not just an accident; it is a consequence of particular ways of life and thinking. Many of us have tried in vain to change this consequence—reading everything we can find about time management in the self-help section of the bookstore or on the Internet. We have also prayed our hearts out. In this book, we will examine its sources and try to find alternatives, aiming for the joy of good timing and offering practical and spiritual advice to those starved for time. We will discover a spiritual reorientation to this time famine that deposits spiritual wisdom into practical alternatives. The spiritual will shake hands with the practical, and the practical with the spiritual, and we will motivate ourselves to feast on time and accept the permission the universe grants us to do so. We will become creatures first and creative second. We will learn that our time famine comes from a deep spiritual debt—maybe even a spiritual emptiness or hollowness. We will stop trying to justify our existence through *activity* and move into the realm of *reflected activity*. We will start feasting on time.

What do we mean when we say we don't have enough time? Why is there such a large time famine in the richest country in the world? How can we who eat so much be so starving for something we actually *do* have?

The chapters belong to each other. They begin, in the first six, with the spiritual analysis of why we don't have enough time. They end, in the last six, with the practical possibilities of getting to enough time. The first chapter discusses the ways we double-time just about everything. Here, I don't mean multitasking so much as trying to please more than one master: worshiping God and Mammon and ending up dancing a two-step that exhausts us.

The second chapter reflects on Noah and his renewal of God's promise. It speaks of the importance of numbers and counting and sizing up just how bad things really are among us time-famished people, advocating a life in numbers and in limitations.

The third chapter uses water as an image for time. Hidden right there in plain sight, rarely noticed or appreciated, we miss the glory by taking water and its flow for granted, as we do with time. There is something wrong when we don't see things as they are. We get hurt.

The fourth chapter talks about intimacy with God and about the many "faces of God"—scriptures and the Golden Rule—proposing that the purpose of life is to love God and enjoy God forever.

The fifth chapter acknowledges that we are in reality people with too much time on our hands, noting that time scarcity is a privilege—a "first world problem." Of course, the poorest among us have a time famine, too: so run around are they from one agency to another, trying to get help; so oppressed are they by misguided people who think their poverty is their own fault. This book looks *from* the first world *at* the first world and its time famine.

The sixth chapter talks about making all things new—or at least something new—and how we doubt we are the kind of people who can be renewed. This is the Easter chapter.

Throughout the book, I talk about *sin*, defining it as missing the mark of our true humanity, being curved in on ourselves or self-obsessed, and being distant from God. By these definitions of sin, I don't mean something small: I mean something large that really affects our days and hours and minutes. I also imagine a beautiful repentance where we turn toward cohesion and clarity as people. By *God* I mean something larger than ourselves; some call this Creator, Jesus, breath, Yahweh, Allah, or the force at the heart of the matter. There is no need to keep God in a Christian cage to address the time trouble from spiritual and spirited windows.

The second set of six chapters focuses on the practical expressions of these spiritual windows. I try to keep us off the *how* for as long as possible because some of that pragmatism is at the root of the spiritual crisis around time. I also respect the pragmatism and try to be spiritually pragmatic and pragmatically spiritual. You could decide to read the book chapter by chapter and understand my privileging of the spiritual, cultural, and economic sources. Or you could read chapter 1 and chapter 7, then chapter 2 and chapter 8, and so on. Take your choice. And above all, take your time.

Chapter One

Why Don't We Have Enough Time?

Very few people feel they have enough time, and many people feel they are time famished. It is the rare, blessed individual who has found his or her way to time sufficiency—much less time feast—spiritually as well as materially. Have you ever heard someone give thanks or praise for being time hungry? I have. These are people who have not only accepted the conditions of the time famine but learned how to live at peace within them. Instead of being spiritually bothered by the material reality of time scarcity, we learn to love time and its sufficiency. We stop whining about not having enough time. We learn to swim in the time we do have. Some of us even trick the time famine into being time abundance.

We have so little time that we don't even have time to find out why we don't have enough time. But it is possible that there is plenty of time, that the universe has already made all the time that ever will be. Here I offer an expensive luxury: a deep look at why we feel we don't have enough time, when it is likely that we have all the time there could be. There may be plenty while we experience scarcity or enough in the places where we feel there is not.

You might amortize the cost of this luxury over the rest of your life and find that it is a bargain to get to the roots of the time famine. If you were bothered by a fly most of the night, you might buy a good flyswatter. If you were lost every day on your way to work, you might locate a global positioning system (GPS). You might imagine your way to where you want to be instead of passively being annoyed at how much time you were losing to being lost. Think of this book as a spiritual GPS, helping you find your position on the globe and in its time and space—and how much of it you have. You are finding your way, your trail, your path, and your position. You are coming to terms with your own time in the larger world of time. You may also find your own space in the larger world of space. You may give yourself permission to find your own version of the *here and now*. When you grant yourself permission to be here in the now and now in the here, like a mortal instead of an immortal, you will begin to feast on the here and now rather than condemning it for being too small, too cramped, too insufficient. You will learn the meaning of the word *enough*.

TWO REASONS WHY YOU DON'T HAVE ENOUGH TIME

The first reason we sense insufficiency rather than plenty when it comes to time is that we have death incompetency: We no longer know how to die. Folk people, who lived in more homogeneous societies, may not have had as many choices as we do, but at least they knew how to die. These cultures knew how to die, and these people died like their cultures, whether in a native tribe or a Ukrainian village or the Italian section of Greenwich Village at the turn of the twentieth century. Of course, some people thought and behaved differently than their culture but for the most part, when it was time to die, they knew what to do, what to say, where to go. They lived life knowing about death, and they were not surprised by it; it was a fact of life and their culture helped in coming to terms with it. "I lived in a country were dying was taught to us from childhood," said Svetlana Alexievich in her 2015 Nobel Prize acceptance speech, speaking of her upbringing in Soviet Belarus, a place and time where death visited in deep and affecting ways. "We were taught death." Death is still taught by more homogeneous or folk cultures, but in complex and diverse societies we have let the subject become neglected.

The first reason for our great sense of insufficiency is we *know but don't know* that we are going to die. We abnormalize death when it is actually a fairly normal, natural, inevitable occurrence. This book is not about death; it is about time. But the two are deeply connected. Many moderns and post-moderns still use the phrase "My time has come" to refer to death. Those who believe they won't die—or that if they will, it won't be for a long time—are just too optimistic, and people as optimistic as they surely don't die. And no amount of reason or emotion or both will convince *Americans* and other first-worlders that we too will die. Forgive my cynicism: It comes from a deep love of my country and how good it could be if it could get over itself. This book is about how great we first-worlders could be if we remembered how to live in time as opposed to thinking we were superior to it. It is about a great love of this American land and its lush spirit—and my dismay that our spirits have turned grabby, as though the Hudson River that spines my space or the Catskill Mountains that constitute my nativity aren't enough just as they are. We seem to always want more, especially if we don't look within ourselves long enough to see our time tension, our contentment casualty, or our peace poverty. We distract ourselves endlessly, but if we stopped relying on such distractions we might be the richest people in the world both internally and externally. I know: these are first world problems; but I am a first-worlder. I know all these problems well enough and painfully enough that I am ready to confront them in myself—and with you. I'll even pay in the coin of time to get to the bottom of my bottom. I don't want in any way to disparage the time famine of those who have to work ninety-six hours a week just to pay their rent or use the one computer in the house at four in the morning as they work to get their high school diploma. The time famine is real, no matter your social or economic circumstance. I know the time famine as a first-worlder and write as one.

The next country we conquer need not be somewhere across the world; it might be instead the nation of the inner, even if that land is innocently considered "eternal sunshine." The main reason we fear death is that we fear our own insides, our own folk cultures, and our own ordinariness. We fear what is at the bottom of ourselves so much that we rarely explore there. But if we could find a way to tame our inner fear of limits and death, so much good could happen. The spiritual route to having enough time is knowing that we have limited time. We were born that way. We are not better than those we conquer: We are just as human as they are, just as mortal as they are, just as flawed as they are.

Best-selling books like Atul Gawandi's *Being Mortal* alert us to how much folk cultures provide by way of ritualizing and normalizing death. One contemporary project—the Living Mortal Project led by Jesse Soodalter, a fellow in hospice and palliative medicine at the University of Chicago Medicine—aimed to understand and influence the ways we think about mortality. It featured—in January 2015—a man "walking into Midway Studios on 60th Street carrying a satchel. In it was a bronze cast of his mother's head: a death mask. He was on his way to a public workshop on death and the kinds of artifacts we keep to remember our dead—belongings of the deceased, art made from their hair, albums filled with photos." He would have been considered normal once; today he is strange. People scatter the ashes of their dead pets but have very different relationships to their own burials or those of their loved ones. A conversation about the funeral often begins with questions—lots of questions—about where to put the remains of the person. Most people know where to put their pets. But more people scatter those ashes or bury them than visit graves of their ancestors. We no longer have ritualized, culturally clear ways to die.

"The Living Mortal Project is in part a response to the modus operandi of the US health-care system. Death is a biomedical reality—and a costly one. 'We have been on an incredibly steep curve' of using technology to defer death, says Soodalter. 'We're really heading very rapidly toward a crisis.' Roughly 25 percent of Medicare spending is for patients who are in their final year of life" (Kott, "Mortal Thoughts"). We would not work so hard and spend so much if we were prepared for death, but we are so afraid of death that we try to buy our way out of it. The Living Mortal Project is developing a scale of death competency; greater death competency would bring with it greater time competency and greater life competency: A lot comes into focus—especially how we use time—when we know, casually and realistically, culturally and psychologically, that we are going to die.

In her 1997 memoir *The Wheel of Life: A Memoir of Living and Dying*, written after a series of strokes, Elisabeth Kübler-Ross reflected, "Dying is nothing to fear. It can be the most wonderful experience of your life. It all depends on how you have lived." Kübler-Ross became famous for helping people see that grief has stages, restoring folk culture to many who had lost it. When we return to our roots in folk culture and our roots as living mortals—created as living mortals, never meant to be anything but living mortals—we will be overwhelmed by the fact that we have time at all. We will feast at its table.

The second reason we don't have enough time is that we try to worship both God and Mammon simultaneously. Our notorious exceptionalism makes us do this: We are so optimistic that we think we can do, be, or have it all. Of course, we can't do, be, or have it all—but we intend to try on behalf of Mammon and against God. We are double-timing ourselves; it has become a way of life for us and the lie against our creatureliness is at its core. Our very optimism is killing us. There is nothing wrong with optimism, but it doesn't explain everything, including the limitation of death and suffering. Optimism protects our innocence about death; we become afraid of suffering when suffering and loss are inevitable.

I will return over and over to the important text from Luke 13 about how you can't worship God and Mammon. For now, just note that it is a mean text, a hard text, one that has a lot of important context around it. You can't fully worship God and fully worship Mammon; that's what it means. You will do much better with Mammon if you put God first. You will do much better with Mammon if you understand what it is in the first place. And you will do much better with God if you understand how good God is. God is not a judge but a joyful creator of your being. God doesn't want you to perform. God wants you to live in praise for all the good things you have been given.

The roots of the pervasive time famine—that feeling that we don't have enough time—are culturally, economically, politically, and psychologically systemic. The three verbs—*doing, having*, and *being*—function as the three commandments of our culture: We are to do, be, and have it all. The four adverbs—*culturally, economically, politically*, and *psychologically*—define Mammon and its grip on us: Culturally, economically, politically, and psychologically, we are to have, be, and do it all. The commandment to increase is Lord. No wonder most people are exhausted. Instead of imaging ourselves as children of God—one who created us to be true humans, like the true human Jesus was, the limited one, the one who even chose limitations—we imagine ourselves to be true gods. We aren't.

Let me take Mammon's adverbs one by one. *Culturally* we are addicted to a certain superiority: Our can-do attitude will make us better than the rest of the bums, and our positive attitude will allow us to achieve positive results. But just the opposite is true: This very superiority fantasy keeps us starving for our humanity.

Economically, there is our sneaky pal capitalism, who is, among all the other -isms, our award-winning enemy. We love growth so much so that we don't know how to *not* grow. We don't know how to love the stage and the state we are in. We always want to be blossoming and never seeding. Here, the 2008 recession comes to mind, when we discovered that banks and bankers were living so much in the short term that they had given away the store in mortgages that could never possibly be paid off. We are good at beginning things and not so good about ending them. We are better at saying yes than saying no.

Politically, the state argues that we are (or should be) self-governing as a democracy when in fact half of us don't bother to vote because we don't have enough time for it. Widespread voter apathy—turning to anger in this season as I write—is injuring our hope in democracy, if not our hope in ourselves. We don't want to spend the time on citizen participation. We know that we don't know enough to self-govern. Instead we look for people to run things for us and allow groups with euphemistic names like Citizens United to buy elections. As our despair deepens, we cross "being citizens" off our to-do lists. We give up on self-governing because we can't handle the self-management. We know each other and ourselves way too well. We "don't have time" to participate.

Interestingly, many efficiencies are proposed for democratic participation. But we all know that the powers that be won't allow online or universal voting. They have too much to lose. You might imagine that people in a democracy would take on questions like this, but they won't because they can't and they—we—know it.

We also have limited understanding about why we allow other people to control us. One is: "Money rules"; that's why we worship Mammon with such vigor. The other is: "You can't change City Hall," which proves to be more and more true. If these things are true—or, whether true or not, if they have invaded and inhabited our spirits—then we have more than God to attend. We imagine we are not creatures if we don't have money; thus, we worship money and accuse God or "somebody" of setting things up in that despicable way. There is a lot of displacement around our impotence around time. We imagine we can't do anything about the time famine, but we can.

Psychologically, we have internalized our culture's commandment to be positive, grow, make money, and "succeed." We hit ourselves with our own sticks. We self-debilitate. These four versions of Mammon so preoccupy us that it is the rare weekend retreat into sports or church or zoning out when we are reminded to sing Alfie's song. What is it all about anyway? Is this all there is? Is life nothing but running and achievement and being busy and being watched and being judged? Is life really all about the money? And if so, who needs it?

After the weekend respite, on Monday we go back to give Mammon its due. We try to do it all, eat it all, have it all—and the very word *all*, internalized, oppresses us into a unique first world problem: the time famine.

We live under the chains of FOMO—fear of missing out. Other people have real chains, which we ignore, some of which come from our very gabbiness, so self-obsessed are we about the fear of missing out on some of our doing, being, or having. Our real chains derive from fundamental spiritual confusion. Self-absorption hurts us much more than it helps us. How else could social media and the Internet come to own so many of us so fully?

Of course, we can't worship both God and Mammon. We can't have a smorgasbord every night, especially if we want a properly proportioned meal every now and then. Some choices have to be made along this road where we are exceeding the speed limit to get somewhere we don't really want to go or don't know if we really want to go, even if we knew where we were intending to go. Confusion prevails about life's destination. The fascinating truth about Mammon and our forced friendship with it is that we don't have to be this way. We have lots of choices, and all we have to do is make them—but to make better choices for ourselves we need to "get down" and fish in our own bottoms to find out why we don't make them often enough.

PERSONAL FORGERY

Choosing feast over famine involves facing our own spiritual forgeries. We can learn to fake it less on behalf of Mammon's multiple and multiplying suggestions, its tendrils tied all around us. We can say we are not okay when we are not okay. We can fool ourselves less. One of the great privileges of being a first-worlder is the capacity to choose. We don't have to be bound to Mammon to enjoy the privileges of Mammon. We don't have to self-oppress.

My favorite forgery is the way I obey the cultural instruction to be both a cosmopolitan and a local, a city mouse and a country mouse, an important person and a regular gal: to both excel and to be a part of the common lot. My second favorite is how much energy I have. Often we fake how strong we feel. I used to joke all the time that I once could to do the work of three people but now I could only do the work of two. I was only half kidding. Why did I brag so about my doubleness? Who was I trying to impress?

Becoming truthful is the antidote to forgery. It is naming which versions of Mammon own you. Are you really only working this hard for your family? Is your marriage really so great that you want to spend time with your significant other or partner? Do you really like the job or do you just put up with it? What about your commute? Is the world you support working for you? Or are you starved for time, and therefore for hope? Do you sense that you have it all—and that *all* might be less than what was advertised?

Much of the truth we apply to our personal forgeries—and yours may be less than mine (and I hope they are)—will be muddled. You and I live in the real world, where we might not have the choice to buy houses closer to our jobs or food that doesn't require gasoline or packaging to get to us. What's worse, we could lose the stuff that comes with our privilege very easily. Why would we want to do that? We live in a complex world, and most of us spend most of our lives attempting to obey both God and Mammon. The time famine cannot be tamed by willpower or optimism; they won't work. What will work is being truthful, if to no one else but ourselves. We may never be fully free of the time famine, but we can free ourselves from the lies we tell to accommodate it.

Without being sneakily optimistic—after condemning optimism or false hope—I will begin to introduce some possible positions that are less fake and more truthful. Feminists often offer a "both/and" instead of an "either/or" mentality. We want to be expansive even though we fear that we can't have it all. And you don't have to be feminist to want to have it both ways—to have both intimacy and work, children and a great job, solitude and lots of friends—which we can't. But we can be less judgmental to ourselves by wanting to have it all—remember the triumvirate of do, be, have—while also being morally wonderful, capable of saying no to it all while not judging ourselves for not having everything. We begin by saying that our participation in what hurts us is a mistake: a spiritual mistake. Our power not to participate in things that hurt us, such as the time famine, is also spiritual power. It means moving in with that almost whimsical God who sticks with us no matter how often we fail to dance on the sacred altar. We cannot have/do/be it all—and that is okay. We regularly miss the mark of our true humanity; we could hit the mark more often by understanding that less is actually less, not more. Making choices about time means there will be less of everything and more of something else, like peace.

My new favorite word is *hybrid*. It may appear that I am nostalgic for the homogeneous cultures of yore, which at least taught us how to die, but I am not. I am joyful that we are mixing it up with each other and that we are migrating toward a magnificent diversity. But I think we have not yet caught up with how to manage time in these marvelous new heterogeneous cultures.

Hybrids are strong, ecologically and spiritually. Hybrids are strong in evolutionary terms. Everyone knows a mutt lives longer than a purebred. Thus I commend my own "both/and" attitude—while I am simultaneously dismayed by its results. I will never stop worshipping Mammon. I can't. That is a very different place than do/have/be it all. It is a place of not having, not being, not doing it all. Simply by adding my intention to be more godly and less trapped, I have changed constant forgery into small honesty. I can begin from there to be glad for time; glad to be created, not always creating; glad to not have to compete with the divine or please the divine so much as enjoy its spirit, which dwells even within me.

A hybrid is different than a fraud because it internalizes some core personal rule. I choose the Golden Rule. You may choose another—but unless you make some choice about what is more important to you than Mammon, you will remain time famished. Why defraud yourself about yourself? Why not remember how much it hurts people to be defrauded, snookered, tricked, and bamboozled? Why self-bamboozle? Why not love your neighbor as you love yourself, and love God above all? Why not make choices about who and what to worship? You may find it easier to be honest with others than with yourself. You know how much it takes to be truthful. You don't want to hurt the people you love by being dishonest. Maybe the reason we marry and love and care for each other is that we need that place of intimacy where, no matter who you are or where you are on life's journey, you can be honest. There is a moral and golden responsibility not to mislead. Telling the truth is the only way not to be the phony you fear you are. You will find yourself in odd compliance with the Golden Rule if you can love yourself even though you know how phony you can be. The question about the love of self in the Golden Rule is important. When we love ourselves, as well as our neighbor, we become more capable of telling the truth to both ourselves and to each other.

When telling the truth to yourself about yourself—that you are a two-timer when it comes to God and Mammon—imagine saying: I am choosing my days and my ways; I am choosing not to advance in my career because I know the eleventh commandment is "Look busy"; I am living the life of my dreams. Or, alternatively: I am choosing to advance in my career and not care for my family as much as I might want because I don't know what else to do and because my fear of not advancing is hurting me; I am just too scared, or too weak, or too injured by what happened when the landlord threw us out when I was a kid. Either way, the very truth, self-told, may make you free. You'll stop complaining about how little time you have and start using the time you do have more truthfully.

Imagine being the master of yourself instead of the servant of Mammon, or even the servant of others. Many of us refuse the arduous task of self-definition and truth-telling because we think we live for others. We do not. The Golden Rule, which Jesus named the best, encouraged us to love God first. Jesus's ideal humanity was the way he loved God first and then neighbor and self in a secondary, even flowing way. Imagine one master—yourself—obedient to God; you as agent and executive of your life, with God as your only master. It sounds so old fashioned, doesn't it? And yet it is a feast of authenticity, lived by the grace of grace and not the works of grace. Less is not just more. Less is indeed also less. Imagine all the time you could buy back from yourself in worry alone. Most of us worry our choices and agencies to death; this worry occupies all the time we don't give to God or Mammon. Becoming clear about who is worthy of worship and who isn't relieves a lot of worry. Less is focus. It is not worry-free focus, but it is a decision to worry less and to *be* more. Freedom is the ability to choose your own master and to master yourself. Freedom was what God offered in creation. It's amazing, really.

Those of us who hope we can approach the optimal good before the end want to aim for good, not just *less bad*. We are tired of the higher math, which brings us so low. We know we live as moral hybrids, as spiritual amateurs, as living mortals. We want less so much that we would pay a lot for it. Oddly, the cost is very low when it comes to living by grace: We simply have to buy into our obvious limitations. We have to stop two-timing God. We have to stop lying and accepting the lies in which we were born.

CLEARING THE SPIRIT

If you grew up in a liturgical tradition, you know Psalm 51 by heart. It is the song for the offertory, sung every week as the money comes forward: "Create in me a clean heart, O God, and renew a right spirit within me" (Ps 51:10). It is what David said when Nathan the Prophet came to him concerning his dalliance with Bathsheba. It is about the most common kind of lie, adultery, in which we not only break the promise of our vows but also take up with someone else as though we were promised to him or her. We basically split ourselves in two.

Many people who have experienced adultery say that it wasn't the affair but the lying about it that broke their heart. Children do a lot of experimentation with lying; it is normal for children to lie. They lie to protect themselves from things they wish they hadn't done: taking money out of a guest's pocketbook or signing up for a hidden text account or not eating their lunch. They are not only protecting themselves from adult punishment or disappointment; they are also protecting themselves from themselves. Most lying is a protection from ourselves before it is protection from the Nathans in our lives, who might know more about us than we think they know.

Thus the old language in Psalm 51 makes sense: It asks the God who finds out about us through the prophets to not cast us away. We want to be held close even after we have lied or become in some way (in the old language) unclean: "Create in me a clean heart, O God, and renew a right spirit within me. Cast me not away from thy presence and restore unto me the joy of your salvation." Zen Buddhist author Norman Fischer, in his Zen-inspired retranslation of the psalms, translates the word *clear* instead of *clean*. I like this because the language surrounding *clean* is basically an old version of sin—one that no longer works in the age of soap and washing machines and much more sex-positive attitudes. The psalm is about the restoration of a right spirit, which usually involves a clearing as much as it involves a cleaning.

This parallels the way we think about sin: We don't think we are unclean so much as that we are unclear. We are without aim, without direction. We aren't even sure there is a God, so it doesn't bother us much if we feel distant from the divine or the ultimate. We might admit to worshipping Mammon more quickly than we would admit to worshipping God, because we really don't know much about what worshipping God would mean. I am arguing here that it means accepting a huge gift, the gift of grace, from a God who created you for the fun of it, and who decided you'd have limits on your fun and your time. It's as if somebody has offered you a new convertible—clearly and cleanly sitting there in the driveway, yours free and clear—and you feel so guilty about taking it that you decide to take an extra shift working for charity or for your family. (Activists are just as capable as capitalists of workaholism: same song, different station.) God effervescently creates us—and we just can't believe it. God creates us, as one poet says, for the "bubbles"—and we flatten the landscape into hard, self-justifying work. We cooperate with the systems Mammon has developed to keep us in line instead of putting our hearts clearly against them. I know it is not easy to give Mammon a hard time. Mammon has extraordinary rewards and punishments. Mammon also steals your time from you and pretends to own what it does not—you.

Traditionally Psalm 51 has been used as the offertory, accompanying the produce to the altar. In bygone days the priest would take his share, and no one ever had to have a capital campaign—because they worshipped in tents. When we put Mammon in its appropriate place—as magnificent material reality the equivalent of magnificent spiritual reality—we make an offering to God in response to God's grace. There is no need to hate Mammon or make Mammon a devil; there is just the need to love the material world of time and place in spiritual as well as material ways. The body is simply a map of the soul; we are psychosomatic realities. There are not two realities, material and spiritual; there is only one reality that is simultaneously both material and spiritual.

What the psalm tells us is that personal forgery has been around for a long, long time. Why do we have to get clean or clear every week in worship at the offertory? Because after worship, we regularly go back into mistaken appreciation of Mammon over spirit. Folk people also felt the need for a cleaning and a clearing for a very long time. They easily ritualize time and its changes. They are taught how to do this by the seasons and by their culture's connection to its past.

We are not the first people who need a refinishing, a restoration of our original shine—a trip to the furniture shop to have our joints repaired or our countenance lifted.

We are not the first people to come into a time famine with a sense of frozen fear or inner twistedness, tangled and snarled. We know what it means to be all mixed up and to imagine our intestines in a tizzy. It may be less dramatic than adultery, but being split in two—or three or four—parts is pretty much the human condition.

When we clear the spirit, we learn to think spiritually and materially at the same time. We learn to think theologically about the life that God has created in us, even though it is short and too focused. The deeper, more foundational reason for the time famine is actually theologically systemic: We still think we can earn our own salvation, security, and safety. We believe Mammon's lies about the importance of the external and we neglect the internal. We are willing to hurt others and ourselves to keep from glimpsing the grace and gift of our creation. We get God's purpose in the universe wrong. We get *God* wrong. We starve ourselves, while God is desperate to feed us. We worship at two altars, God and Mammon—or, if you don't believe in God, the best self and the self who needs to pay rent, the presented self and the self who does stuff alone, the made-up self and the one who forgot her lipstick. We even see the splits in church. My congregation, Judson Memorial Church, likes to say it is the best church you can't find—the perfect church for imperfect people—and we are also *mostly* the church we wish we were: the church of our website, not our coffee hours. Being split into lesser and greater parts is the human condition, not the human exception. We are hybrids, and hybrids are often very useful to evolution, especially if we evolve.

Sin is actually a very helpful word. It is not something "those other people" know; it is not somebody else's problem. It is something we know in our own lack of time. How dare we say God didn't give us enough time? Martin Luther said sin was being "turned in on yourself" (*incurvatus in se*). We each imagine that we have the lead role in the world's play, but this can't possibly be true. What about the millions who came before us and the millions who will (hopefully) follow us, or even the ones with whom we share the earth right now? The earth groans under our self-obsession.

Others say that sin is missing the mark of our true humanity. We behave in ways that demean our creation. Ecological integrity could achieve the aim of our humanity or assure a clear miss at our target. Ecological integrity understands the relationship between body and soul, God and Mammon, spirit and matter. It is like a wholeness of self, in which we make choices about time, from a centered place. Ecological integrity is missing from the planet and its people. Restoration of that coherence is the way we have enough time.

Still others say that sin is distance from God. When we aren't intimate or in primary relationship with the divine, we aren't dirty so much as distracted. We can't worship both God and Mammon, but we sure try. Distance from God is idolatrous: Second things become first and refuse to be dethroned.

Imagine how restored our salvation—and God's creation—would be if we were clear and less focused on ourselves, more intimate with God, and more fully human.

To resolve the time famine within us, we need not fuzziness of heart, but clarity of heart. The time famine really does hurt us. It keeps us fuzzy. It keeps us too busy to get clear.

Chapter Two

The Importance of Numbers
Sizing Up Your Time Trouble

Numbers have a bad reputation. People often say the numbers are just the "numbers." We discount them as if they are less than the real truth. We scoff at their definitiveness. We don't like to think it is 2018 or 1918, or whatever slice of whichever century we happen to be in. We like to think of ourselves as larger than time, even though clearly time is larger than we are. We live outside of the big seasons instead of fully in the small seasons, the seven to ten decades of spring that we actually get.

I know a man who bought a six-thousand-dollar stove. He was convinced it would fit into his kitchen. It did not; that's why he has a six-thousand-dollar stove in his study. We may discount numbers but we also mismeasure the amount of time or space we actually have.

I often measure the amount work I think I can do in one day, only to find my estimate off by at least two or three exhausting hours. I think I can speed up, but in fact I often slow down, so overwhelmed am I at the fact that my numbers, my count, just didn't add up. In the end, subtraction of my energy is the result of my false addition. It might even be a *forged* addition, in the sense that I am worshipping at the altar of multiple masters: my own magnificent creatureliness and limitation and my own optimism and idolatry. Aren't I Godlike? Most days, I mess up the numbers of my creation. I often imagine that next spring will be plenty soon to plant that garden I really want or to spend time with that friend I miss. Procrastination is my middle name, telling me how richly I have learned to live in the time famine while mythologizing it as expansive time.

I am not alone; many others live here. Many people, when asked, say that all they'd really like is one more hour to each day. I think that is probably the Sabbath hour, the one that collects all the rest. This Sabbath collection is

13

available, but you have to stop working at the twenty-third hour, not the twenty-fourth. Numbers are important.

Numbers are an access point to limits, and limits are an access point to mortality. And mortality is our friend, not our enemy. On any one day on any one trip, everything may work out just right: The temperature may be perfect, the bugs, small in number, buzzing only for about ten minutes right after sunset, when the host's dogs are in a good mood. Or it may not: It may be insufferably hot and buggy, and the dogs may not have be fed at the right time so they try to eat what dinner we could save from the flies and drink what wine we could save from the mosquitoes. Things go well when we live in the season where we actually are, instead of in an imagined one. If the season is a buggy one, then we adapt to the obstacle of the bugs. That's authentic. When we live with bugs as though there are no bugs, that is illusion.

On a recent trip to Costa Rica, I had a big "seasoning" lesson, a lesson in the importance of what many call *timing*. Timing, the folk wisdom tells us, is everything—and it is true. Timing is all about numbers. It is numbering the seasons and the likelihood of seasonal days. It is being in season. It is knowing when to quit, rather than getting home way too late on a Saturday night to enjoy the next day. Our errands have to be disciplined or our leisure passes away.

Different seasons require different kinds of margins, time to attend to the boiler or the snow shoveling or the mosquitoes. Even on a vacation, different seasons involve timing. Seasons are not famine; they are feasts.

Let me tell you the tale of two labyrinths—actually, the same labyrinth, but walked in a different season.

On that night in Costa Rica, we had a perfect evening. We walked the world's largest labyrinth at La Senda, near Tamarindo in Costa Rica. We arrived at 3:30 in the afternoon, just as the hundred-degree heat began to subside. The clouds kept the heat of the sun off our backs, and the mosquitoes didn't like the near shade. As the sun began to set, the monkeys in the trees began to howl. When we returned to the compound, where a three-course meal had been prepared for us by our eco-hosts—the people who ran the ecotourism project—the table was set for our party of thirteen; glowing candles alerted the nearby meadow of our arrival. There were no flies, despite the meadow and barnyard full of pigs and chickens and geese. There were no mosquitoes. The peafowl were bedding down for the night and had eaten all the bugs, including the ticks that might otherwise have bothered the five barking dogs. Not a bug drowned in my wine glass.

Our friends who had taken us to the labyrinth walk said the previous month's guests had not been so fortunate.

One guest was their seventy-five-year-old mother, who doesn't care for dogs. They had arrived a half-hour late to the labyrinth walk and stumbled into the cactuses in the dark on their way out. They had seen no monkeys. The dogs kept jumping up onto their laps during the meal. The mosquitoes were everywhere, and when they weren't swatting the mosquitoes they were removing the flies from their red wine.

The labyrinth was the same, but it was walked at two different times and so the walkers had two different experiences. In real estate we often say location, location, location; in life, we might say timing, timing, timing. In fact, if we were to combine the two—time and space; timing and location—we'd have a pretty good understanding of why a spiritual GPS is important. We could constantly locate ourselves in time and in space, as people who actually *belonged* in time and space rather than as people who *managed* time and space. Surely it is not a crime to arrive an hour late to something. Being late may be a way of being in time rather than off time or out of time. But sometimes being late causes us to miss the seasons. When we say we want to feast on time, we often mean we want to season time with taste. We want to get the seasoning right: not too much and not too little. Think salt and how it can enhance or overwhelm.

Time and space are meant to be dwelled in; they are not meant to be managed. To be sure, we can manage them to some degree. We are, after all, agents of our own lives and self-managing as a species. But many of us overdo management and underdo dwelling, and this becomes our idolatry and our downfall.

What I have said about clearing our way to and for grace is mostly a matter of acknowledging timing. Some things are wonderful in summer but not in winter. The more deeply we can live inside time rather than as if we were outside of it, the more able we will be to accept our inevitable and eventual mortality—and the more fun we will have on the way to it. We will always know about surprises, including the surprise of death. The more aware we are of our death or our diminishment, the better able we will be to deal with both, when the time is right. Awareness gets our timing right. We will not be surprised to discover that not every walk in the great labyrinth of life is a happy one, and we will be ready for those that aren't. We will also know the meaning of the great circling, what Rainer Maria Rilke called the "growing rings" in him that cover over the rest of him. We live in our history as much as our present. Rilke's imagination of himself as a tree with rings of age is a lovely clear thought. It places him in time, dwelling slowly.

A church in Costa Rica has a sign advertising itself that says, "Why didn't God tell Noah to leave the two mosquitoes off the boat?" Good question. There is an answer, which applies to flies as well: ecological integrity. Without flies we wouldn't have birds and without birds we wouldn't have butterflies and without butterflies we wouldn't have flowers. Likewise, mosquitoes. Similarly, Rachel Carson argued frequently that bug spray was something the "control guys" came up with to manage time and space, which can't be managed, to drive all the uncomfortable stuff out. She was right about bug spray, and her analysis extends to the time famine. There is just no way to get rid of all the bad stuff. It belongs here. As Thich Nhat Hanh and many Buddhists (and Christians) argue: "No mud, no lotus." No trouble, no growth; no sadness, no joy. Ring by ring, we grow with both pain and pleasure as our partners.

The widespread time famine so many of us experience comes from over-management of time. It comes from the control guys, so deeply internalized in all of us. God did not tell Noah to keep the mosquitoes off the ark for good reason: They are part of creation, just as limitations are. Oddly, limitations are the gateway to the best art. It is often the biggest obstacles that an artist uses to create something fully of its place and of its space. The great architect Lewis Mumford said he built his best buildings around obstacles in the land. Oddly, to dwell in time, the best thing we can do is follow Mumford's way and head straight toward our limitations.

Our goal as human beings is to be of our place and in our space, to be in the here and now. We have a gift of three score and ten, maybe more if we are lucky. Some of us don't get that much; some get much more. Appreciating the gift of what is, rather than trying to have, do, or be what isn't, is the trick to abundance in time. Think of this book as an advanced placement course in appreciating where you are instead of needing to be somewhere else. You live in time and place ecologically with integrity. Environmentalists call this *ecological integrity*: taking only what you need from the earth in any one season rather than using up its resources. You don't belong someplace else; you belong where you are.

Humans are distinguished from other animals by our self-consciousness and our ability to make choices. When we choose to disrespect the numbers of time and space, the latitudes and longitudes of our lives, we live outside the mark of our true humanity. Missing our mark is a kind of sin, one that isn't punished later, in hell, but now by the presence of hell and its entanglements in ordinary time. We let the time we do have pass us by. We forget our timing, or we act as though we are above timing. We become seasoned instead of seasonal. We have flavor. We taste good and our taste is good. We walk the second labyrinth rather than the first. We show up on time and we don't complain about the bugs if we fail to show up on time. We belong to the bugs and they to us. Noah and God had their reasons for bugging us. The reasons have to do with our seasoning, with keeping us above trapped or confused, as though we live with an advanced understanding of our placement in life.

VINING AND UNVINING

Respecting our numbers, whatever they are—whether fourscore and ten, or less, or more—is key to living seasonally as well as living rhythmically. We live in stages. Consider the older woman, trying to be a weekend athlete, who pulls her hamstring on the first day of the tennis season. She is likely not looking at her age. (Yes, I have done this, and lost six good weeks of the summer to my pride.) I am likewise sometimes amused by fifty year olds who tell me they are "getting old." There needs to be some number level fact about how old we really are. We need be to less in our perception of that age and more in our realization of that age. That really helps with the time famine. When people think they are complimenting us about our age—telling us we don't look that old or that young—we might say that we are proud of looking our age and living our age.

My thirty-year-old congregants often complain that they are not "there" yet. By *there* they often mean some career situation they have long pursued. They work very hard to get there and then when they get there, they often find out that there is less than they had hoped it might be.

Gardeners understand. In the fall, we have to pull up all the stakes we pounded in. We have to untangle the vines that have wrapped around the fences and each other. Most of us love planting; unplanting is a pain in the neck. The tomatoes scratch. The tendrils tickle. The sticky green stuff—which is my favorite weed because it is so prolific—hitchhikes on our jeans to the next patch and finds a way when there is no way. It is a survivor.

In the fall many congregations prepare for the annual ecumenical Thanksgiving service. There is nothing more environmental than this annual agricultural and culinary festival. We really do thank the spirits for harvest, home, and all that is safely gathered in. We let the late afternoon light go and are more seasonal than usual. Winter can drag on; spring can be abrupt in its arrival and departure; summer is for the long day. But fall is not something you can miss. It is an environment with its own calling card: "Hello, I am here. The days are shorter now."

We also find ourselves more interreligious in this season. Some think of environmental religion as pagan. I think it is postdenominational, beyond any one kind of God. We go way back to go way forward. We live in deep time, seasonal time, developmental time, and stage-friendly time. That time is a feast. It is like a Thanksgiving feast for everyone at the table: All is safely gathered in.

Humans, however, seem to know how to use our marvelous consciousness to ruin just about everything, including Thanksgiving. One scene—which really did happen in one time and place, but is universal in the way it both comes together and flings apart—may explain it: the ecumenical planning committee for the Wednesday night community service. Everyone agrees to invite a Native American person to do the opening prayer. They vine and twine around each other in consensus about the opening.

One person says that he hopes the one praying won't find a way to condemn the rest of us for stealing his people's land in the opening of the service. Another agrees, saying that the reconciliation moment, a ritual or remembrance of the wrong that was done, should come later in the service. A third argues that it is such a happy day, with all of us being together and all, that we should really avoid the past and move on. Let the one praying do what we all will do: Stay in the vanilla environmental zone of praise and thanksgiving. There is no need to worry about the tendrils that vined around the front fence and took off some of the paint. We have the harvest; let's not fuss. Mosquitoes may show up, but we'll just hope they won't.

Remember how hard we try to keep the bugs off the ark and out of the wine?

Imagine a world that was safe enough for its own truth about things that happened to Native Americans, or things that you yourself have done that you wish you had not. Wouldn't you be in less of a hurry if you stopped running away from some past or running toward some future? What about living with the truth about yourself and about your people? What would happen if we became the kind of uncontrolling people who lived with rather than against that which bugs us? Wouldn't we have more time? Doesn't it take extraordinary energy to live outside of seasons, without bugs, without memory, without forgiveness? Isn't the great brush-over of reality—living outside of time and outside of place—part of the reason we feel so starved for time?

There are no instructions in the harvest hymns about how to handle this matter—"All is safely gathered in, ere the winter storms begin"—but there is plenty of instruction from the environment and in ancient texts. The coming together and the flying apart, the warm and the cold, the inner and the outer are all connected. When we give thanks for the good, we also give thanks for the bad.

The good and the bad are pieces of each other, as Zen Buddhists argue about compliments and complaints. In a compliment and a complaint, a difficulty and goodness, we are just looking at different sides of the same coin. In the Buddhist notion of praise and criticism, in both instances we are dependent on the outsider to confirm or negate us.

Evan Pritchard's excellent book *No Word for Time: The Way of the Algonquin People* explains more about cycles than clocks. Pritchard argues that the Algonquin live seven years at a time in their consciousness of time. I have less concern about time in our little Thanksgiving planning tableau than I do about how we "clock people" learn how to cycle and learn—or relearn— the capacity to engage planting and harvest, joy and difficulty, at once. These matters are as connected as seed and harvest, vining and unvining. (To contrast native culture with Western or European culture, Pritchard's work may be read alongside Mark C. Taylor's *Speed Limits: Where Time Went and Why We Have So Little Left*, Juliet Schor's classic *The Overworked American: The Unexpected Decline of Leisure*, and Arlie Russell Hochschild's work on the second shift or time bind.)

If I were planning that Thanksgiving service, I would argue for a mixture of repentance and thanksgiving. I would argue for a true harvest of bountiful time to enjoy and be, no matter what has happened. I might even go and pull out another tomato stake while humming, "We gather together, to ask the Lord's blessing, to hasten and chasten . . ."

How does this connect to paying attention to the numbers, and the bugs, and timing? It has to do with letting a little difficulty into your thanksgiving. People who feast on time are not without difficulty; instead, they are people who are not trying to run away from difficulty or banish it or outlaw it. They allow for bugs. They refuse to control the astonishing gift of time. They learn how to receive as well as how to grab or consume it. They single-time instead of double-time.

When we single-time instead of double-time, we get back all the time that we have given to worry. We single-time because we don't want to worship God and Mammon at the same time. We want to rely consistently on God's grace, which says we have a chance even if we did steal the land from the Native Americans, especially if we stop lying about it. Neither time nor land really belongs to us. They are both gifts. The truth, everyone says, will make you free. I think that freedom is feast amid famine. It is also single-minded.

NOAH'S ARK AS A GUIDE

When the flood began, the normal cycles halted. Perhaps they had already been thwarted and ignored, and the flood came precisely to call forth a conscious understanding that they had stopped. Similarly most of us would agree that in modern times—when most Americans have trouble sleeping or work twelve-hour days or eat out of paper bags while driving—the normal cycles are in danger.

It is funny that the instructions for packing the ark are so precise. Bill Cosby once had a funny about asking God what a cubit was. Noah's ark is a story rife with numbers, the sacred geometry of the forty days and forty nights as well as the seven days of Creation featuring prominently in the story. It is almost as though God were reestablishing normal cycles, after a breach of covenant, number by number, limitation by limitation.

According to Rabbi Arthur Waskow:

> The Bible says that just before the rain began to fall, there were seven days while Noah's family and all their passengers sat waiting in the Ark. The rabbis

teach that during those seven days the sun rose in the West and set in the East. In other words, the seven days of Creation were being run backward and so the sun reversed itself. During the precise solar year that all the animals and humans spent aboard the Ark, the rabbis also say they all refrained from sex and thus refrained from initiating the life cycle.

When Noah wanted to test out the dry land, he tried to restart the great cycles of night and day, death and life. First he sent out a raven, black as the night, named arva, a word similar to erev, "evening." Then he sent out a dove, white as the morning, named yonah, a word similar to yom, "day." The raven, bird of carrion, cleared the earth of the dead carcasses that were the end product of the last life cycle before the flood. The dove brought back for food the olive branch, the first new life that had sprung up after the great disaster.

Noah's effort to renew the cycles won God's response in the Rainbow Covenant. God's promise to renew and preserve life mentions precisely the timely cycles through which life renews itself. . . .

What are we to learn from this? In the age of Modernity, the sacred cycles of time have been thwarted. We have let our desire for "productivity" destroy our sense of holy time and holy cycles. We have become so drunk on our new ability to produce goods that we have forgotten to rest, reflect, contemplate, meditate, and celebrate.

We are out of whack in time. We often don't even sleep long enough to dream, and God loves to show up in dreams. Most of us know we are out of whack—we at least tell that truth to ourselves—we just don't know what to do about it. And we fear, fairly constantly, that some kind of ending is upon us, something the size of the flood.

"This hyperproductive mode, in which time is only a raw material for management, has taken us to the brink of ecological destruction. In a world that discards meditation and celebration as a waste of time," we dare not be surprised at our upside-downness, our out-of-whackedness, our sense of foreboding at what might come next. Very few of us will really be surprised at the next catastrophe.

"Noah's own name means 'the restful one.' Only a restful one can save all life" (Waskow, "Rainbow Sign"). Those who learn to rest will learn to live, and will learn to be thankful and grateful for time, including the trouble embedded in time. Rested people might be more useful than unrested people, just like Noah was. But we don't rest to save the world! We rest to rest. We rest because God's gift to us is rest. We don't rest to be more useful unless we want to become more firmly the property of the four horsemen of the modern apocalypse: the cultural, economic, and political commands to be exhausted on behalf of growth, psychologically internalized.

Oddly, what the ancient wisdom and the ancient one told Noah and his family to do was to take care of animals. How many of us today see our lives as connected in any way to that task? Doesn't that also seem like a waste of time? *Really?* we might ask. *Assure mosquitoes a life?* But why *wouldn't* that be a highest priority for the wise and the grateful—just as the wise and the grateful might invite the Native American to the table to say whatever he or she needed to say? Why do we worship at two altars so often? Isn't that double-timing the true waste of time? Why try to please the master of truth and the master of control—or the master of truth and the master of false harmony—at the same time? Why do we do that? We are hedging our bets. And our bets won't hedge.

EASTER TIME AND NATURE TIME

In early 2016 the BBC reported that Justin Welby, the archbishop of Canterbury, was discussing the establishment of a fixed date for Easter with Pope Francis, Coptic leader Pope Tawadros, and Ecumenical Patriarch Bartholomew of the Orthodox Church. I can't tell you how upset this makes me. The feast in time is about living in nature's time, not the calendar's time. Nature has one set of numbers; the calendar, another. Nature lives in both kairos and chronos time, in the same way that you and I are spirited bodies or embodied spirits. You can wear a watch, but you can't live by it; you have to live a larger way than just the way of the watch.

The Vatican approved a proposal for a fixed date for Easter in 1900, subject to agreement among other Christian churches and governments, but no agreement has yet been reached (BBC News, "Archbishop Justin Welby"). I understand why it might take more than one hundred years to reach agreement on a matter as important as this one. I am rarely conservative, but on this matter I can't believe Pope Francis and I are on different sides; his entire encyclical tries to reground the world in natural principles and cycles—and then he takes our biggest day and gives it to the calendar people. The calendar may be full of my friends the numbers, but it is full of them in static, unnatural ways. A fixed date for Easter will hurt those of us who are trying to learn how to feast on and in time.

In Western churches, Easter is the first Sunday after the paschal full moon that occurs on or after the vernal equinox; in simpler terms, the first Sunday after the first full moon after March 21. This has been so since the Council of Nicea in the year 325. Although the paschal and full moon, the ecclesiastical and the astrological, actually can vary slightly, March 21 is used as the official day, and Easter is always on a Sunday; if the full moon falls on a Sunday, then Easter is the following Sunday. Thus Easter—based in a lunar cycle, not a chronological one—can occur anywhere between March 22 and April 25.

A favorite subject of discussion each year is how "early" or "late" spring is. In any hardware or convenience or grocery store, you can chat someone up at length about this subject. The darker ones refer immediately to climate change; the lighter ones argue that "it's always late" or "it's always early." Of course, what is "too early" or "too late" is completely relative to the last couple of days of weather (for the subjective) and to weather records (for the objective). Time is never too late or early. Seasons differ every year. They like doing that. We could join them in enjoyment of time's variations.

I would say that Easter was much too early in 2016. It was nearly as early as it could be, falling on March 27. I prefer a more natural cycle, with the earth warmed up a little more, the last snow not still threatening. I would prefer the daffodils out, and not just the crocuses. I would prefer to think about planting as opposed to protecting things that foolishly emerged off-kilter, spiritually and naturally. These preferences of mine are of no interest to nature or the divine. But I enjoy having them, as a way to live in the rings and the circles of time.

I don't know how people are supposed to move to pastel clothes or Easter bonnets with the weather still so uneven, and I don't know how you have an Easter parade with high winds up and down Fifth Avenue.

But all these objections are minor. They are a nod to the secular, a bow to the chronological, with its major offense to the kairotic.

Chronological time plods along, minute by minute, hour by hour, on the human invention called the clock. Kairotic time jumps up on your lap like a puppy and says, "I'll have a walk now"—or a life-changing thought, or a terrible pain in my chest now. Kairotic time retains a sense of mystery. Kairotic time is always bugging you, like a watch that is too tight on your arm. You're late. You're out of time. You're behind time. You're too early. You were in the wrong place at the wrong time. Or you were lucky: you were in the right place at the right time.

If we are to retain any sense of mystery about Easter, we're going to have to refuse to manage time. We are going to have to substitute sacred numbers and sacred seasonality for secular numbers and fully owned and bought seasonality, the kind that gives us jingle hell starting before Thanksgiving. We are going to have to move through the numbers of life with a flow and not with a force, living fully wherever we are rather than forcing ourselves to reach a certain stage by a certain age.

"My time has come," said Jesus on the night of his betrayal in the garden by his friends. This is kairotic time. They thought it was just another Passover, like the one year before and the one that was coming next year. It wasn't. It was the Passover after the first March full moon. It was a time out of the time that could be managed.

Please join me, metaphorically, in telling my friend Pope Francis not to make an Easter mistake by giving it to the clock! Or just delay a couple hundred more years. We could delay for the right reason and just stick with seasonality as our approach to life. You are delaying for the right reason. You are sticking with a season and not folding to an unseason. You are vining and timing, locating and being in line with longer seasons, more ancient patterns. You are finding a time and a place in which to dwell.

MISSING OUR MARK

When we refuse to number our days and our ways correctly, ignoring the power of the mosquito or the fly in the ointment, we end up trying to do too much. We vine when we should be unvining and unvine when we should be vining. We lack seasoning, which is so much better than aging. We go active around time—numbering our days seasonally, with great flexibility—instead of remaining passively interested in it. Yes, some activity is good and helps us dwell in time, but too much activity misses the very mark we are trying to achieve.

One version of sin, as I have said before, is missing the mark of our true humanity. When we don't have good numbers for our days and our ways, we are almost always out of whack, off base, upside down—involved in a form of destruction of nature. You may not have the time to care about the big floods, far away from you. You may think they don't matter to you or connect to you. But that is the second big version of sin speaking in you: *incurvatus in se,* or self-obsession. There surely is a way out, and it has to do with "so numbering our days that we come to wisdom" (Ps 90:12). Water may be able to show us a way, especially if kairotically understood.

Chapter Three

What If Time Were as Important to Your Life as Water . . . and You Didn't Know It?

You may agree with my assertion that living in the time famine is a form of sin. Your participation in the time famine might miss the mark of your true humanity. It might cause you to curve in on yourself in endless self-obsession or keep you from intimacy with the grace of God. Your very refusal to number your days accurately becomes a mortality-denying practice that plummets you from feast into famine with regard to time. But I certainly hope you know enough to know about sin that when it is acknowledged, there is a glorious forgiveness awaiting.

Here I want to lighten that load a little bit and invite you to join the human race. You are not perfect. You are not unlimited. You are not immortal. I am with you in being imperfect, limited, and mortal. It is not a crime to be these things—but it is a sin. "All have sinned and fallen short of the glory of God," said St. Paul (Rom 3:23). Imagine turning from sin and getting to the glory! Imagine the turn toward glory and away from the trudge! Imagine focusing on the second part of the sentence—the glory—and leaving behind the first part of the sentence: that everyone, including you and me, has sinned.

Oddly, glory is hidden in plain sight, beneath the choices we make against it. Like forgiveness, it longs to flow over us and clear us. Forgiveness is like that great feeling we get after a good shower. Here, I want to show you that time is an invisible gift, like water, and how simply seeing it might turn us toward flowing in it.

TIME IS LIKE WATER

We imagine that water is plentiful, cheap, and fully and forever at our disposal. It is not. It is not plentiful, especially to poor people or people in developing worlds, who must walk miles a day just to get enough to soak beans. It is certainly not cheap if Poland Spring or Pellegrino get involved. And it is internationally threatened by population explosions, climate change, and the interest of corporations in selling it and making it an ever more scarce commodity. Bottling water is not a giant sin, compared to other commodifications—but it *is* a sin.

We who are rich enough to not worry about water are actually poor in time. Those who are poor and have to worry about water have more time, even if much of it is spent in getting to water or other basic supplies. The rich and the poor experience the time famine in different ways; some people, especially women, walk miles a day to get water for cooking. They don't put a bottle in their purses and sip when thirsty.

The word *Orwellian*—coined to describe the way the powerful misuse language—comes to mind: Things are not what we say they are. The idea comes from George Orwell's book *1984*, in which the government is all-powerful but completely illogical. It refers to a world where the rules are unclear and horrendous punishment can befall you at any time for actions you didn't even know were forbidden. This world is very confusing, and you wonder if you know what is going on. This is one aspect of the time famine: It does a bit of gaslighting. We aren't clear because we are genuinely confused, perhaps even confused intentionally by people who benefit mightily from our confusion.

Gaslighting is

> a form of intimidation or psychological abuse in which false information is presented to the victim, making them doubt his or her own memory and perception. The classic example of gaslighting is to change things in a person's environment without their knowledge, and to explain that they "must be imagining things" when they challenge these changes. The term derives from the 1938 stage play *Gas Light*, in which a wife's concerns about the dimming of her house's gas lights are dismissed by her husband as the work of her imagination, when he has actually caused the lights to dim. This is part of a wider pattern of deception in which the husband manipulates small elements of his wife's environment, and insists that she is mistaken or misremembering, hoping to drive her to insanity. ("Gaslighting")

Eventually she goes crazy and stops trying to manage her world. Eventually, many of us stop trying, and say idolatrous things like "That's the way it is" or "That's just the way things are."

We believe we are creatures of a loving God. We trust that grace is extravagant, covering even our propensity to refuse it and to worry it. We know that we live in the large seasons—summer, fall, winter, and spring—and also in the small seasons, from birthday to birthday and genome to genome in our seventy or so promised years. But we also know that there are bugs, and we are bothered by them. We know that we don't get it. And we fear that some of us are manipulating others of us, and that we are letting them do it.

What if we are so gaslit or so manipulated by the Orwellians that we misunderstand what is really important, like water or time? What if we think they are something that they are not? Would that be a mistake sufficient to scare us into different behavior, or would our great capacity to rationalize pull us through? I fear the latter and note it in myself. I also know that I miss a lot of reality because it is just too painful. I rarely come to that language I want for myself—which is "I am living the life I want"—or to a world where everyone has the water they need.

I once met a woman in India who walked ten miles each day to get water, carrying it in a large bucket ten more miles back to her family. I was so affected by her—by her life and by my own faucet and shower at home—that I became obsessed with water. I can't stand to waste water, so instead I "waste" a lot of time using and reusing water, empting the water from abandoned bottles in the park onto plants, saving water in buckets, and the like. I am not really wasting time; I am appreciating it and the woman I met. I don't need to be so obsessive about water; I choose to.

We misunderstand water as much as we misunderstand ourselves. We manipulate others into imagining that untruths are true. We misunderstand the big stuff—like water and time—so easily and so frequently that we might be just a little scared about the problem of the time famine. Misunderstanding our own abundance or our own scarcity is a fundamental problem in the time famine. It is not a small one. It is the kind of problem that deserves a good, solid nervous breakdown, or at least extensive rituals. Instead of either of these, I recommend moving into the big seasons: the kind that water enjoys brook by brook, stream by stream, river by river, ocean by ocean. I recommend looking into the great underground and noticing that God's intention was a graceful flow of water. Why not live there instead of inside the convenience of a portable water bottle? That ode to convenience is actually costing you your sanity and your truthfulness, a little of your money and a lot of your time. When time and water are bought instead of exchanged, when the buyer is more powerful than the seller, big trouble ensues. That's what happens with the water bottle. Use it as a way to enter into your sin. You and I might be bought too. That truth, recognized, can be great news, but denied, it can be awful news.

PORTABLE WATER BOTTLES

Portable water bottles are the kind of convenience that actually causes inconvenience; they are Orwellian that way. A friend of mine described her addiction to alcohol once this way: "I don't drink much, but that other person, not I, when she drinks, drinks a lot." We may think we are better than we are in our use of water or our use of time.

I don't use many plastic water bottles, although every now and then one ends up in my hand at a party or an event and I realize I am hooked into its world. It is not hooked into mine. My world is full of hopes; its world is full of sales.

Why carry water? Why make water portable? Why ship water from Maine to New York? We have fantastic water in New York. I don't care how much better the water is in Maine. It just makes no sense to ship it to us. My church's refrigerator is filled with Poland Spring water bottles. And we really don't mean to be such sinners. We just don't know how not to. We live in a culture of convenience. That very convenience, designed to save time, actually costs us a lot of time, in worry, fear, and anxiety. Water bottles per se are not sinful; it has to do with how and why we use them—as well as their damage to the sea.

Why not repent our use of water bottles in a regular, ritualized way, one that allows forgiveness to wash over us and new life to come? When we see the symbol of portability for what it is—a technology that encourages us psychologically, culturally, politically, and theologically to do, be, and have it all—we can make the decision to *not* be portably convenient. We can go out of our way to not be portable or convenient.

I may argue that store-bought reusable water bottles are equally obedient to the cultural economy of portability and therefore only "less bad" as a practice. Drinking water out of public fountains or at home from a glass may prove to be radically disruptive actions. Will they change the gaslighting from the corporations that wish to sell more water to us—or will they change us into people not stupid enough to keep buying it? No. But such an action is a claim to time feast. It is a way of saying, "I prefer to be less convenient, not more convenient; less portable, not more portable. I prefer to be a creature who lives in abundant time, in my season and in the larger season of the world. I prefer to be a creature who sees what is going on." This small change is actually a huge one. Time is always there, flowing like water, and we usually don't acknowledge or see it. The reason we may dare lighten up—even become comic—about our sin is that the changes we need to make are so very small. They are almost like turning and looking in another direction. They are not enormous: simply a change in the way we look and what we look at, the way we acknowledge or don't acknowledge the realities hidden in plain sight.

Right now, in the third and fourth world, Nestlé is buying up streams while arguing that water is not for sale. Nestlé needs to be publicly shamed, regularly and often. We should never shame a person; people who live more seasonally should not trash those who may be on a different place on the spectrum of personal change. But we do have good solid fights with robots and corporations; they don't deserve human feeling. Nestlé is not a person. It is a corporation. It thinks like a machine, not like a human being. Nothing else will stop it from commodifying water and doing to water what it tried to do to breast milk. The time famine is not an accident; it is a corporate intention, and people can rightly shame corporations for dehumanizing us.

Real people need help abandoning their toted waters. They need to be rewarded—not confused or made to feel small—for not sinning. Corporations like to make ordinary people feel small for wanting to do good instead of just doing less bad. What is good is withdrawing permission from the Nestlés of the world to tell you what to do and how to do it. Withdrawing that permission is as simple as not buying their bottles. It is also that large. It is turning into living right side up rather than upside down.

If we are able to lean toward decent use of water bottles and tote water in reusable containers—if tote we must—and more importantly, if we understand that we are making this change for a large reason, if in a small way, major changes will result. We will be in less of a corporate-driven hurry. We will be more in a human water-like flow. The industrialized ocean will find a fighting chance. Spiritually dehydrated people will drink, in tears of hope, from the sea of their lost and dissolved anger. There is spiritual liberation, as well as material improvement, in liberating ourselves from water bottles.

In what kind of universe would we not prevent the wars we could before they killed us, or our children? How could we not have enough time to face reality? According to Pope Francis, "The control of water by large multinational businesses may become a major source of conflict in this century" ("Encyclical Letter," sec. 31). Only people who have been snookered and who agree to be snookered can't see realities like water and time famines.

To resolve the time famine, we need to move beyond religion that dehydrates and supports economic practices of dehydration, and into rehydrating spiritual practices. Portable water is actually a big sin, not a small sin. When we are not able to wash out a glass or turn on a tap to get our water because we have to get four places in the next hour, we are missing the mark of our humanity. We aren't perfect. We make mistakes, but we can repent. We can show the world how much we want the good of our creation and that we really aren't interested in compromises or continuum. Transformation is not going from vanilla to chocolate, but from vanilla to music. Water bottles are already moving into the land of yuck instead of yum. Beautiful hand-carried water bottles that use water out of faucets are a "delightable." They can be inconvenient as well as delightful. That is not a small thing. That is a large thing. Delight and beauty often war with convenience and hurry. Making decisions every now and then for delight and its consumption of time and effort can show us that we worship God and not just Mammon.

I know it is not always apparent how the small things connect to the large things. Sometimes they are so small they make us feel stupid. But when we compare how stupid we feel for never having enough time, and if we dive deep enough to answer the question of *why* we don't have enough time, things change. We see that small is large. We notice that convenience is unsatisfying, even hurtful to ourselves. We see that portability helps corporations much more than it helps us. We wonder why our intimates are turning down the lights in order to trick us. Why would they do that to us? We remember that water is not for sale. And a light goes on inside us: Neither are we.

The Lakota speak often of a healing of ancestral wounds. Nothing less will resolve the time famine that our parents taught us, thinking it would make us happy and wealthy and wise. It did not.

We who are rich are actually poor. Water, which seems free, is not. We live in worlds or words that don't describe reality. Thus, when we think of being pressed for time, we have to wade through densities of reality. How can people as well off as we are be pressed for time? How can free people find themselves caged? How can a loving God allow people to gaslight each other? Did our own parents gaslight us? Is our boss gaslighting us? Did our teachers or our SAT scores gaslight us? Why did they do that?

The reason is in the bugs, somehow. And I don't think we can get rid of them without getting rid of something important about us. Is the time famine necessary, then? I think some of it is. But do we really have to sin more so that grace may abound? St. Paul asked that question more than once. He seemed to have understood the human condition very well.

OUTSIDERS UNDERSTAND THINGS DIFFERENTLY

I don't think people who are free of the time famine are necessarily any more moral than other people. Many people who drop out of the world because the time famine is too much for them, choosing a simple life in order to live a personally more safe life; they feel less endangered by convenience and hurry. That is surely more moral than living an unlived personal life, one without delight or its companion, freedom. But the real purpose of understanding our creation is to notice how our drop connects to all the other drops. We are not in this for ourselves. We are in this to enjoy God and praise God forever. We are in this for the glory of being fully alive and not blocked, whether Nestlé is blocking us or we are blocking ourselves.

God is the kind of parent who likes all of us. Pope Francis wrote, "Unsafe water results in many deaths and the spread of water-related diseases, including those caused by microorganisms and chemical substances. Dysentery and cholera, linked to inadequate hygiene and water supplies, are a significant cause of suffering and of infant mortality" ("Encyclical Letter," sec. 29). Even people who are too busy to care don't want babies to die. They think they have more compassion fatigue than they do.

In Orwellian terms, we imagine that the material world is much more real than it actually is. It is surely real and beautiful and magnificent. But to be more clearly spiritual is not to engage in competition with the natural world and order so much as to refrain from idolizing it.

We are led to believe we will starve if we don't bow at the altars of portability and convenience. We won't. The opposite is true for the majority of people: More people will live in scarcity if we don't attend to each other and to each other's truth.

We hear the phrase frequently that people have "drunk the Kool-Aid." This joins gaslighting and Orwellian mistruths in keeping us off balance. When we drink the Kool-Aid, we buy into cultural realities that may or may not reflect our true values. Culture gaslights us. We live in ways that people like Orwell point out, as though lies were true. When off balance, we participate in our undoing. Again, St. Paul: "The Good that we would do we do not and the evil that we would not do, we do" (Rom 7:19). We believe things that cannot possibly be true, if there is a good God and if people have the capacity to be godly, which we do.

There is a water way beyond this kind of complicity and duplicity. It comes at baptism, or perhaps in another water ceremony that marked your entrance into the world. You don't have to be Christian to be claimed by God. Baptism is one claim, saying that you have no other lords but the one claiming you near birth or when you make your choice to live in a certain way. When we have children, most of us don't want an Orwellian or gaslit existence for them. We sense ourselves at our very best with a new child. We want clarity and goodness, good weather and good water. We affirm a way forward. Why would we not want to be a child over and over again, or finally to have a chance at that widely fabled "good childhood"?

AFFIRMING BAPTISM

Baptism is a sacrament, an outward sign affirming an inner grace. It means you belong to God and not to Nestlé. According to Ched Myers, in the Christian tradition we speak of baptismal waters as the symbolic source of renewed life. That metaphor, however, is predicated upon a broader biblical vector concerning "living waters." The prophetic literature contains a recurring eschatological promise of social and environmental restoration through the "rehydration" of the world, a rich tradition worth exploring for ecological theology—and for those of us on the luxurious journey toward time sufficiency and time feast.

"In our historical moment we cannot talk about 'waters of renewal' without first acknowledging the systematic 'dehydration' of the earth by industrial civilization. Of the many specters of our deepening ecological crisis—climate change, species extinction, peak oil, declining natural fertility—one of the most pressing is 'peak water.' The Pacific Institute's Peter Gleick describes this as 'the critical point, already reached in many areas of the world, where we overtax the planet's ability to absorb the consequences of our water use.' We see its symptoms in global desertification, widespread water insecurity, and declining water quality" ("Everything Will Live"). We are powerfully mystified by how the water in Flint, Michigan, could have had so much lead in it. We know trouble is coming, but we don't really have time to pay attention. And so we attend what we mis-attend with anxiety about time and mortality, life and its actual meaning.

In this chapter I have been arguing that our denial about the water crisis is the parallel of our denial about our time crisis. We know that water is essential and yet we mistreat it or ignore it or act as though it is not that important. We are also in denial about the time crisis and frequently rue its loss. Water and time are in the same kind of crisis, big enough to warrant the attention of people who care but inaccessible to us because the very time we don't have keeps us from acting. Besides, many of us blame ourselves for having a time famine. We do indeed participate in the time famine, but it comes from forces outside of ourselves—like the water crisis—in such large measure that we have to be very careful not to self-aggrandize or overestimate our power, which will only result in failure of a kind that keeps us more captive over time.

Follow the parallelism of our twin denials about time and about water—pretty big subjects all alone, much less twinned. Our ancient ritual of baptism reflects a modern ecological fact: Without water, there can be no life. Peak water, like the other grim trends, represents an endgame unless we "turn around." This should compel Christians not only to urgently seek earth literacy but also to reread our Bibles from the perspective of the "groaning creation," as did Paul in Romans 8:21–22. Water is a good place to start. Though we in the first world take it for granted, it is likely to be more important than oil, as the years groan—or glory—on. There could be more glory than groan, especially if our awareness about water and time becomes more clear.

"Waters shall burst forth in the desert, streams in the wilderness; torrid earth shall become a pool; parched land, fountains of water" (Is 35:6)—this is a vision of feast. Indeed, all invitations to feast on water could also be issued to feast on time. We are invited into the grace of the material matter of water. Water is spiritualized consistently in the scriptures. So is time. Both are now being reduced to their material nature by clocks and by people who want to control our time, whom we allow to control our time. But both water and time are spiritual and material realities simultaneously. They are never just one or the other, not even in baptism. They are both sacraments, material signs of divine grace.

John the Revelator acknowledges the ecology of grace: Water is a divine "gift" (Rev 21:6). "Let the one who thirsts come forward, and . . . receive the gift of living water" (Rev 22:17). Here John appropriates another subversive promise of Isaiah, which envisioned an end to the commodification and privatization of water by the powerful: "All who are thirsty, come for water, even if you have no money" (Is 55:1). I might paraphrase: Let all who are hungry for time come and receive the gift of living or inspirited time; let all who thirst come for time, even if you have no money. Neither time nor money is for sale. Amos appeals for "justice to flow down like a perennial stream" (Am 5:24). There is justice in people's being released from the time famine, just as there is in fair distribution of water. When God transfigures the world, the waters will flow abundantly again. There won't be a flood. They will be in right relationship to the human need. Things will not be off-kilter; they will be on-kilter.

Our lands are not parched by science or nature. We parch them. Our time famine does not come from our individual sin; it comes from our consent to Mammon's rule over us.

(For more on watershed theology, see Ched Myers, who works with Bartimaeus Cooperative Ministries in the Ventura River watershed in California; http://www.chedmyers.org.)

MYSTICS AND REALISTS

For resolution of the time famine within you, you will have to see things that you do not see right now. They will have to pierce your heart. Maybe you don't mind the time famine. Maybe you are interested only in your water and not in Flint's water, or about the larger issues the time famine demonstrates. Maybe you are well acquainted with your own mortality and still fear for the future of earth and its streams. And maybe you care only about how to get hold of your own time because you are overwhelmed by larger social problems.

Some of us are mystics, some of us are activists, and some of us find the freedom to be both. Like that lively marriage between matter and spirit, action when married to reflection is beautiful. It constitutes the glory.

"Both" is the destination and the mark of our true humanity. We are to be richly connected, simultaneously, to spiritual and material reality. We are not to privilege one over the other but to hold them in a beautiful, life-giving tension. Nor are we supposed to care only for ourselves or only for others; instead we are to care primarily for God. We are not supposed to be thirsty or scared that we don't have enough time to be fully human. We have been created with the capacity to be both mystics and activists, both passive and active. It is sad that so many of us have become either antimystic or antiactivist, thereby stranding ourselves far from the glorious streams of action joined to reflection and matter joined to spirit. We are missing an understanding of time as time passes us by.

Mystics enjoy both those deeply comfortable with questions and those who want a few answers. Mystics sing life in a different key. Mystics are loners who proudly protect their inner space—and usually, when they have one of these profound experiences, they find themselves thrust into a sense of oneness. Mystics are not the best community members—and at the same time, those who don't have the capacity for mysticism are horrible community members. They flatten things. Because life *as it is* is so important to nonmystics and antimystics, they tend to say things like "That's just not how things are" or, shrugging, "What are you going to do?" They may also say with pugnacity, "That's just the way things are." A typhoon flattens the Philippines and the antimystic says, "What are you going to do? That's just the way things are." Yup, and there will be more of them. In a meeting, the antimystic loves to say, "That won't happen" or "We can't do that." Antimystics power themselves with a presumptive reality engine. These are also the people who love to tell you that they weren't surprised by Occupy's failure to bring heaven to earth in six months. They are people who want a plan and who believe most causes don't have even a prayer.

Mystics are different. They join Robert Bellah in a definition of religion, that it is nothing more than the imagination of another reality. While both mystics and their opposites live in what Sadie Smith calls "narrative claustrophobia," one lives there alert, while the other lives there confused. Mystics let a story claim them every now and then; realists refuse to let a narrative claim them. Before I give my pitch for mystics, let me first affirm and acknowledge realists. If you are more realist than mystic—and believe me, all of us in this narrative claustrophobia just have tendencies to one direction or another; there is no pure type—you deserve appreciation. You have made your peace with the world as it is. For you, an encounter with what is *real* is crucial: Just give me the facts, please. You want to see more clearly, assess with greater refinement. You not only want to know what is going on, you think you *do* know and you calibrate your activities and your emotional response accordingly. You don't think you are right so much as you think you are real. You sleep better than mystics do. You probably have an exercise program as well as a budget. You manage, and you manage well. Your feet are on the ground. You give perfunctory thanks for water. You vote for the right people. No one ever calls you a "loose cannon." You have made your peace with the great numbers of life and know how to keep your nose clean. You are not gaslit. You see—but what you see is limited to what you *can* see. You are less alert to other levels or dimensions of reality than mystics or religious people are.

Mystics are more likely to be bumpy in our approach to life. We see new heavens and new earths everywhere and jump on their bandwagon ineffectively. In fact, *ineffective* is our middle name.

Let's go straight to what is weird about religious types of people. We do sort of believe that God created us, that Jesus sustains us, and that the fruits of the spirit are everywhere, or we are familiar with the doctrine of our own Jewish or Muslim or Buddhist or whatever faith. We live by grace and not by works, and we believe that within every death there is new life. We also resist spiritual correctness with every bone in our body. We resist it the same way we resist political correctness. We insist on the right to believe or not believe in our own way, with the same vigor that someone might run the half marathon. We are almost predictably reactive in our capacity to question each other. We pray to be able to see. We pause often enough to look around. We acknowledge that we have been snookered and have participated in the snookering—and passively consented to it.

Prayer is a source of renewable energy, and mystics can't help themselves. If the words *prayer* or *pause* bother you, think instead of *thinking* or *reflection* or *looking around*. Mystics like to look deeply. They just have to find time to pray. Simone Weil calls prayer absolute unmixed attention. Robert Frost says, similarly, that a poem is a momentary stay against confusion. Prayer goes to the quiet corner of the party and listens. Prayer gets rid of the stale energy. Prayer unpacks the boxes slowly and lives as though it has all the time in the world. Prayer is the mystic's habit. It is like a wheelbarrow that lets you make the heavy light.

For water to be saved and safe and enjoyed—for time to be saved and safe and enjoyed—we need to marry the mystic to the realist, the material to the spiritual. It will be so much fun. We will have the pleasure of seeing doubly—as opposed to double-timing—what is happening in time and living there and then, here and now. Glory will be our guardian and our gate.

Chapter Four

Time Famine as a Really Good First World Problem

Climb up the ladder of material success and you will find more people complaining they don't have enough time. Climb down the ladder and you will hear the opposite complaint. From "I don't know where the time goes" to "Just killing time"; from "I can't hear myself think, it's so loud in here" to "The afternoons sometimes are just so long"—the laments shift. Rare is the person anywhere on the ladder who finds time a good costume in which they fit: It's too baggy or too tight, too abundant or too scarce.

Families with two working parents, children and pets, mortgages and cars probably have the most justification for their sense of time insufficiency. How *could* they have enough time? They have an industrial-age school system in a digital age, plopping their children back in their laps at three o'clock every afternoon or requiring extra services, like child care or ballet or baseball, to keep the kids occupied. Single parents sometimes face all these matters doubly, and those who work three part-time jobs know yet another kind of time famine. All have fixed expenses that require regular incomes, even at the lowest level of the economic ladder. They have the old-fashioned idea of supper, that antiquated notion in which four or five people gather at a certain time to eat a prepared meal. They have psychological pictures of how children should be raised as well as constant adjustments to these pictures that tax them in anxiety and money.

As a card-carrying feminist, I have argued for decades that we didn't need women to adjust to the demands of the economy so much as the economy to adjust to the demands of women. A six-hour day would be so much better for both men and women, but then the insurance companies and the landlords and the banks would not be able to charge what they do. If only men had become more like women instead of women becoming more like men.

37

Something has happened to the economy. It has become very big. It is a
large part of our everyday life. It is not a silent partner in getting food to us
but a loud whistle telling us what to do and when to do it. It has become
almost all we know of Mammon and its constant instructions to us to make
more, go faster, speed up, and consume more. It has dumped its dysfunction-
ality—and its commandments—straight into the laps of first world families.
Families in the developing world are likewise harmed as money gets more
attention than God. We are in a time of great adjustment: economically,
psychologically, and spiritually, we are out of sync. We have not lost only
folk culture; we have lost a culture that is a partner with its economy. Most
people who are economically secure are psychologically and spiritually inse-
cure. We are not supported by the economy. The time scarcity begins and
ends here.

But there is another story, hidden right in the main one. This is the story
of the people with too much time on their hands. It is the story of people in
prison, whose numbers are increasing. The most successful prisoners are the
ones who plan how to spend their days and learn to be disciplined in their
personal use of time. They have little time scarcity, unless you call idleness a
form of scarcity. It is also the story of the third of the people over age
seventy-five in this country who spend their last days in nursing homes.
Instead of the nearly utopian ones, where residents can have pets and plants,
choices about when and what to eat, most nursing homes are more regi-
mented than the army. Why? So the "patients" are "safe." Most of those
patients would love to have an afternoon doing some activity where they may
risk a fall. It is also the story of the many poor people who must spend time
sitting in uncomfortable chairs at the housing authority or the food stamp
center or the emergency room with numbers in their hands, waiting to be
called. If not there, they are trying to find resources for inexpensive food or
transportation. Some of the unemployed even have enough hope to keep
looking for a job, even though they know the job will not pay much and will
destroy their spirit.

Anyone who is unemployed or underemployed knows that looking for a
job is a full-time job. That word *unemployed* is a cause for such shame in our
culture that sometimes when my own church members tell me they are unemployed, they beg me not to tell anyone else.

Poor people lose the time to live happily, without blame or self-blame,
because they have to do the poverty hustle. Many are eloquent in describing
what it means to get to the center that is supposed to help them, only to wait
all day on a line and be told to come back tomorrow. Social theorists like
John McKnight have argued that if poor people were given some of the
money that takes the train home to the suburbs at night in the pockets of
social workers, it would save a lot of money, result in a lot less crime, build
the economy, and still leave jobs for the social workers.

The disabled or differently abled join the old, the imprisoned, and the poor in having too much time. Often the time famine means having lots of unimportant things to do that require lots of important time. Our culture commands us to produce, and those who can no longer produce no longer matter. When the worker takes an hour to get your form back to you as you sit in the waiting room, you experience too much time and feel its wasting. Racism is still another factor: If you are nonwhite and poor, people blame you for your poverty, and many question the ways you use your time and whether you use it productively.

We have a class A human system, involving those who produce, and a class B human system, which demeans and demonizes those who have been actively disallowed from producing.

One of the members of my congregation uses a wheelchair to get to church activities. Her mobility is not completely limited in her chair, but it is highly limited if the elevator is out at any point in her journey. When the elevators in the subway are working, she gets to church; when they are not, she doesn't. Even when they are working, it takes her two hours to get from Brooklyn to Manhattan. If they are not working when she returns, it can take her four to get home if she is able to figure out which elevator might be working. I wouldn't call her situation a time famine; I would call it a form of oppression regularly faced by the disabled. People who are disabled must spend a lot of time looking for assistance, and usually they don't get it. Many give up looking; if they are desperate enough to keep looking, they give up in other ways. They don't kill time; time kills them. People who live in these conditions as second-class citizens—right here in the richest country in the world—have a very different problem with time. Like those living in the second and third worlds, they have time for folk culture, time to talk to each other, and time to develop a way of being. There are advantages to being disadvantaged, but what most disadvantaged people would like is the food and the beds and the freedom the rest of us have to complain about the time famine.

Those of us in the first world have made a choice to have money and not time. Those living in the second and third worlds have not made a choice not to have money; that choice has been forced on them. I don't know if there is a real relationship between my wealth and others' poverty, but I suspect there is. I suspect the root is in the lack of a cultural agreement about who matters. Busy people who work for a living are understood to be better than those who don't or can't. We have a cheap culture, one that values effort and has little empathy for those who can't do. In the second and third worlds, many countries retain their original or folk cultures. When development arrives, that disappears.

One of the members of my congregation is bringing social work to China. She is an accomplished professor at New York University, herself a Chinese immigrant, and has been engaged by the Chinese government to help develop social work curricula for all the universities in the country. She is overwhelmed by this task, not least because she doesn't want to Westernize or "develop" China. She knows that since China has become richer, many elderly people have been abandoned, and they need social workers to help them. She also knows that since China has become developed there is more domestic violence than the folk culture permitted. She knows the need for social work as cultures of care break down. She also wants to keep as much indigenous culture in the social work curriculum as possible, including Buddhist and Shinto points of view about mutual care, but the government has prohibited such inclusion. As the people of China get more money, they will get less time. Notably, that lost time will detract from the ability of people to care for each other.

Another group of first-worlders most oppressed by not having enough time is the sandwich generation: those trying to care for their aging parents while caring for their children. Chinese people are known for simultaneously caring for both their elderly and their children. As the economy of capitalism has a deeper reach into personal life, in both China and the United States, children and elders are the ones who suffer. The people of China are not alone in the excruciating feeling of wanting to have money and wanting to care. No one wants not to care.

What might be spiritually different? How can we find the time to care when we already don't have enough time to "keep body and soul together" or to "make a living" or to "get some down time"? We make choices about God and Mammon. We might choose some material poverty on behalf of some spiritual wealth, although that would be so countercultural that most of us probably couldn't make the turn. Or we might remake community, turning suburbs into collective child- and elder-care centers, street by street. On any given suburban street, there are probably a half dozen disabled people and a half dozen seniors alone all day. Think averages, not facts. Imagine what would happen if those people found each other, and the people who drove off each day in their singular cars on their singular rides to their singular jobs found them. Social innovators are wisdom figures; they are bioneers: biological pioneers. Like the great actress Meryl Streep, who, when she found out that sixteen older actresses were performing in a play, in a small house, snuck her fame in, showed up, and watched the show. She remembered Mama, the title of the play. Streep figured out how to care for people she didn't have to care for. Capitalism often makes us wonder if we should do that or "waste" time on that kind of caring.

We can do what we can with the seniors we know. We can accommodate their culture. We can not blame them for not producing "any more." We can remember what they did give. What all the people who have too much time need is a little thanks for simply *being*.

You don't need to be old to make this work. You might also be a part of that first group of time-starved people: the young families. I had three children, all in diapers for a very short time, but long enough. I took them on trips whenever I got a speaking gig. Instead of taking the airfare to go spout my stuff, I asked for a train ticket, and so I got to take each of them on a train trip around the country, a couple of them twice. I know: privilege—I have lots of it. On the long train trips, I would organize other women my age with children: You take the two or three of them for the morning; I'll take the afternoon. We'll watch each other, but first we'll trust each other. We had socialist day care on Amtrak, all across the country. It was so much fun. I got to look out the windows and relax. Another mother got to look out the windows and relax. There was no need for all of us to be sitting in time famine all the way west or east. There is just no need for some of us to have too much time and others to have too little time.

THE RIGHT AMOUNT OF TIME OR THE RIGHT AMOUNT OF ANYTHING

Psychoanalyst Adam Phillips, in *Missing Out: In Praise of the Unlived Life*, says, "Instead of feeling that we should have a better life, we should just live, as gratifyingly as possible, the life we have. Otherwise we are setting ourselves up for bitterness." He also says: "Don't fuss over life." Phillips pretty much does any damn thing he pleases. Why not? Why do we obey so many orders so much of the time? What amount of time is the right amount of time? How would we know? How would a prisoner or a patient know? The real issue is who gets to say what the right amount of time is. There is a question of authority here. Personal authority is the ability to control yourself; personal nonauthority is giving permission to other people to control you. Even in prison or in a nursing home, you can control yourself.

Philips also discusses D. W. Winnicott's idea of the "good enough mother"—the mother who sometimes responded promptly to our needs and sometimes didn't. On occasion we will be satisfied and on occasion we won't. Why didn't our mother alert us to that? We think we know more about the experiences we don't have, the unlived life, than about the experiences we do have. This is the way we miss our lives. Even our mother can't assure us of the right way to be or not to be; the best thing she can do is share us with the world and the ups and downs and ins and outs of time.

Before she started her exhausting presidential campaign, Hillary Clinton said out loud that she was too tired to know how tired she was. I was so proud of her for telling the truth. It was a dangerous truth, as most truth is. Why would it be necessary for a candidate to become president to be exhausted? Why do we think it is incumbent upon a person in leadership—or a plain old mother—to be exhausted? The reason is simpler than we think: We don't know how to measure time. We don't have the numbers, the big numbers or the personal numbers. We don't have a sense of flow, the way water flows naturally. We expense water and flow on our expense accounts, getting paid or wanting to get paid for just about everything we do. We have outsourced senior care, child care, housecleaning, and more. We haven't seen the face of God, and we imagine that we won't see the face of God or don't even think it is important to see that face. We don't think it is okay to be what we are: humans, creatures of that which is larger than us, people who have no need to be that important.

I respect Clinton's fatigue, and her honesty. She had enough time and space to tell the truth. She didn't know what was enough for her or for us or for her life's mission. Neither do I.

GETTING TO THE RIGHT

I try to call a woman friend every day. I do this because one of my oldest and best friends told me a year ago that she was a "barnacle looking for a boat." I understood. Unlike me, she doesn't have a husband who does just about everything for her. She is alone. She keeps herself busy and beautiful and thin and funny, and she is a barnacle looking for a boat. She travels the world, helping young girls in horrible/wonderful places. She sees a lot of great plays. But she still feels her time could be better spent. She wants to be more connected.

The main thing I have learned in parish ministry is this. Some people have too much time and others have too little. Moreover, some of us spend too much time on things that don't satisfy. We have more buyer's remorse than we know. There is one Sunday several years ago that I want my beloved Judson Memorial Church to always remember. It was December 8, 2013, and we were in the midst of a leadership transition. A man named Brandt Silvers and his family took over the Christmas lunch of Stone Soup. Rachel Tenney, a remarkable daughter of the congregation, was elected clerk. Josh Wolfe, a remarkable son of the congregation, spoke about the capital campaign, while his sister, Megan Wolfe, gave the buildings report. Christine Binder, a nearly thirty-year-old Oberlin graduate, was elected moderator. Ken Kidd gave the nominations report. Ted Dawson stepped down after five transformative years as moderator, focused especially on sustainability issues, the gym, and real estate. It was a generational transformation, good in all ways, but first of all in the optics. Those too heavily feeling the institutional burden gave a sigh of relief. Those whose institutional responsibilities were light gave a strong yes. The true nature of the relationship between those with too much time and those with too little time was revealed: Those who have too little responsibility need to change places with those who have too much, and those with too much connection need to changes places with those who have too little. This balances out our existence in time. Why should some have too much and others too little?

If there is a message to the time-starved part of you, it could be this: Find someone to take your place. If there is a message to the time-abundant part of you, it could be: Take somebody else's place. Grab it. If you are a barnacle with too much boat, release. If you are a barnacle looking for a boat, attach. Wouldn't it be simple to help each other here?

Of course, we could all just continue to starve. But why would we do that?

TRUST FAMINE

Right behind the time famine, as in living in the neighborhood, is the trust famine. It lurks in the back of our minds, advising us not to invite other people into our circle: to allow them to take care of our children on Amtrak, for instance, or to offer to take care of theirs. It tells us that people who have been released from prison are dangerous, even though they were much more dangerous—and expensive—inside, twiddling their thumbs. It tells us that when people are old they have nothing left to give or do or be. Bias against the "useless" elderly is a key cause of the breakdown of trust. People don't know how long they will be valuable or valued. They can no longer fulfill the commandments of do/be/have it all, and all they have left is wisdom. Who needs that?

First-worlders have so much imperialism that we decide to do everything. We are exceptionalist as humans: We think we are more capable than we are. We read our own press releases and believe them. We decide to worship both God and Mammon and end up faking it when we discover we can't. We don't trust the "useless" people, which means we don't trust the useless parts of ourselves.

The meaning of life may be in connecting those who have with those who don't have. It may reside in trusting those no longer useful, anticipating the time when we ourselves will be no longer useful.

I don't mean just useful or even just money. I mean instead our capacity to make choices, being valued as a human and treated as valuable as a human, being able to trust our own aging process, being able to imagine that we are valued whether we are in a waiting room or a nice restaurant. I have often heard from people in jail or who are about to be deported or who are mentally ill that they knew our church couldn't really fix or help them; they just didn't want to be blamed anymore for their poverty, whatever shape it took. They wanted the blame for their lack of privilege off their backs. They didn't want to be told they were poor because they weren't good, or mentally ill because they were bad, or disabled because they had sinned. It is amazing how much power people who can make choices have to develop a contrary culture, a rogue social analysis, and a pioneering point of view. It is also amazing how much difference a smile can make to a person, unfortunate or fortunate. That smile to the useless part of you and your privilege can matter. It can matter a lot. You might learn to trust the people who have too much time on their hands. You might think about all that time on *your* hands. What a beautiful idea: Time is on all of our hands.

THE GOLDEN RULE

You can't talk too much about the Golden Rule. It applies to all of us. The Rule of One—another name for the reciprocity of the Golden Rule—means there is a trustworthy connection between those who have too much time and those who have too little time.

You know how the other religions say this. Confucius said: "Never impose on others what you would not choose yourself." Lao-tzu said: "Regard your neighbor's gain as yours and your neighbor's loss as yours." Seneca said: "Expect from others what you did to them." We can use this ancient wisdom to connect to the people in jail, or on the train, or in the nursing home, or stuck in the elevator. Imagine if your rush was their pause.

By *mutuality* I mean that wisdom implied in the Golden Rule: that first we love God, then love each other, as a way of loving ourselves. In that love and that way, we find all the threads we need. Often called the rule of reciprocity, or the Rule of One, the Golden Rule transcends party affiliation. The Law of One argues that when one is harmed, all are harmed, and when one is healed, all are healed. Theologies of reciprocity reveal that we find our best self in others and vice versa. In this book I argue that while change is good, transformation is even better.

Could it be possible that in the same way we rob the poor of material security, they rob us of spiritual security? Because we can't let go of our wealth and because we can't not care about the poor, we "worry" about them, objectify them, and really don't want to be like them. Sort of. There is not a neat exchange here. Time is the same for all; there is no more time for one than for another. Instead, there is a mandate for trust and exchange, a way to give to the other what we have too much of and for others to reverse the favor. Right now the time famine is pervasive. Everybody has insufficient time. Granted trust, the opposite could be true.

SELF-HELP MOVEMENTS

Theological reimagination about sufficiency is mightily different than a self-help movement. One requires trust; the other requires willpower. In truth, both trust and willpower will help us. Leading with willpower, if it thrusts toward trust, will be magnificent. But willpower is the power of will alone, and it is not enough.

Self-help movements are light, often packaged and frequently digital versions of ancient wisdom. They argue—rightly—that there is a lot we can accomplish by buying costly forms of personal self-improvement: a gym membership, an online course in meditation, a wardrobe makeover, or a decluttered house. They argue—wrongly—that way too much is up to us and omit the graceful God who playfully created and sustains us. They rarely spend much time with the imprisoned or the elderly or the disabled. They go off gospel pretty quickly in ignoring the very people who have the capacity to open our hearts to the wounded parts of ourselves.

So many imagine a God whom we can please by becoming better, but the truth is that "better" can be pulled out of us, for our best selves, by the grace of God. By *grace*, I mean the unmerited and unbearable joy of being alive. What we can do for each other and ourselves is mutual mentoring, mutual encouragement, and mutual education. We can opt out of the instructions that most self-help movements give, which often involve playing harder at self-improvement. Even teachings on meditation and the relaxation response are often dedicated to the art of making us better worker bees. The ecology and economy and environment of the human being have become oppressive under late-stage capitalism. The capitalist system doesn't need fixing, as Ben Cohen of Ben and Jerry's put it so well: "It is already fixed." We can and may learn ways to trick it while trying to fix it. We have choices not to obey these internalized instructions from capitalism run amuck. We can move into a trust feast, or even smile more, or both. We can become aware of how fixed the system is and how we don't want to be a part of the system that hurts us. We can also try to change the system. But the first change is in our internal consent to it. We may not be able to work outside of it but we can definitely live outside of it.

There is nothing wrong with capitalism itself. It may be the best economic system there is, yet it has also flooded its boundaries and involved money and a near eleventh commandment to increase in parts of life where it doesn't belong, like leisure, cooking, and health. The first thing people think of when they get sick is how much it is going to cost them; if health insurance companies didn't make so much in profits, maybe people could get sick without financial anxiety. Wellness is not for sale; neither is healing. But in our world, "health insurance" is a matter of lost control and bankruptcy.

This is a self-help book about helping ourselves in sustainable ways. It does not wear you down but lifts you up. It is a soft revolution and even softer resistance to the rigged economy. It is a kind of magic that doesn't put down the other self-help books and their attempts at making things more beautiful and peaceful, but it does argue against their version of better as being *more*.

Lost to us in modern times is the wisdom figure, descended from the tradition of the healer, the astrologer, the conjurer, or the fortune teller, each of whom has a pre- and postbiblical role. They are our wisdom literature after the light wisdom literature has failed us.

In a world where too much focus is on money, and earning it is seen as a form of bettering ourselves, wisdom figures teach us low-cost personal insurrections and resurrections. We go rogue and renegade and do a lot with a little. We go from "I scratch your back if you scratch mine" and into a covenantal economy: "I like scratching your back, without any need for a reward." We move from the overweening instrumental to the light and lively sacramental. We connect our time famine to those of others, which may come to them as abundance.

We do what the marketing people want us to do: We find a hole and fill it. What is missing for most of us is appreciation and respect, which are what MasterCard would call "priceless." We don't need to hate money or capitalism or the art of the exchange—they are good as far as they go—so much as put them in their place.

Before I could write this book I had to get out of the way of my impotent anger at the system. There are other things that money should not buy. One is health. The other is recreation. A third is happiness. The trust strategy is the connected strategy. We learn to trust those whom we fear and whose suffering we fear. We get out of their way and thereby, in a golden way, get out of our way. There is great mutual benefit when we withdraw our consent to the systems that hurt us. We find ourselves feasting on a little bit of time and a lot of personal coherence.

Getting out of the way teaches us how to stop competing with others and start complimenting them. It fills the hole of the appreciation deficit disorder. As a strategy, it goes the communal route, arguing that there is a lot we can do for each other that costs nothing more than intention and self-direction. The things we need the most can't be purchased or "worked at" or "worked for." They come from the richness of mutuality. Right now, we are mired in a way that is hurting us. We need to get out of that way, and its tentacle ways, to get to the way we want.

Chapter Five

Knowing What's Important

Elemental Approaches to Time

In the modern world, we get to live in two spaces just about all the time. One is real space, where there are chairs and tables, knives and forks, and pictures on the wall. The second is virtual space, where you can talk to a friend in Australia in real time or order supper with a click of a button. Living in two spaces at once creates another kind of time pressure. Most of us like both spaces—we like the solidity of the one and the magic of the other. But we don't have time to be online, and spinning a World Wide Web with our fingers and our eyes glued to a screen and *also* be in real space. For most people today the virtual space is as real as the table and chairs. We live half-time in both places, not full-time in either.

I work on the campus of New York University, near the historic Washington Square Park. The park is a magical, real place. Gorgeous music fills the air from pianos people wheel in or horns they carry. There is an abundance of food, a spraying fountain, a lot of children, and good old-fashioned noise. But these days, just about everybody in the park has their faces buried in their phones. The tourists—sometimes in groups—all stare at their phones, all trying to find directions to their next destination at once. I daresay phones are as much a part of our larger life direction as they are our smaller directions. Students with "ears" march along talking about or to their significant others, saying things much too intimate for children to hear. Toddlers in their strollers are fiddling with their parents' phones. As the child psychologist Jean Piaget said so well, play is the work of childhood. The miniature kitchens or tool benches of yore and the smartphone of today are desirable playthings, even for infants.

How do you live in two spaces at once? What has this doubleness done to our sense of time? For me, e-mail has become so oppressive that I intentionally use notebooks to categorize and make lists of my e-mails, especially the ones I know I will forget. I like to touch the notebooks, just to remind myself of real time. I also use cardboards for calendars. I find them on the streets and recycle them, just for fun, and also just to touch. I don't like to be plugged in for my calendar. I like to think that I am still somehow grounded in time and space, in the elements of life. I may be wrong, but it is at least an interesting fiction.

New work abounds on the problems and possibilities of the virtual world: Judy Wajcman's *Pressed for Time: The Acceleration of Life in Digital Capitalism*, Wendy Hui Kyong Chun's *Updating to Remain the Same*, and Philip Howard's *Pax Technica: How the Internet of Things May Set Us Free or Lock Us Up* are excellent examples. We love/hate it. We hate/love it. We don't want to be left behind or to miss something. And we can't imagine how we are going to keep up.

Interestingly, writers in the past also attended the matter of constant communication and connection. I remember a time when I used to write letters and receive a lot of letters. I knew significant stress about not getting back to someone and experienced great peace when I got caught up on my correspondence. In *Jacob's Room*, written in 1922, Virginia Woolf said, "Whether we gain or not by this habit of profuse communication it is not for us to say." Today this interest in profuse communication has doubled and tripled. The multiplication of online communication devices and tools is unlikely to end any time soon. Almost everyone complains about digital communication— while constantly communicating. We are at the same time much more in touch with each other and much more out of touch with each other—and I do mean *touch*.

In an important article, "In the Depths of the Digital Age," Edward Mendelson notes, "Every technical revolution coincides with changes in what it means to be a human being, in the kinds of psychological borders that divide the inner life from the world outside." We refer to ourselves as "not having enough bandwidth." We borrow technological language to describe ourselves and they turn out to be true. We really don't have enough bandwidth for all the worlds available to us. In Thomas Pynchon's 1973 novel *Gravity's Rainbow*, the narrator says, "Temporal bandwidth is the width of your present, your now. . . . The more you dwell in the past and future, the thicker your bandwidth, the more solid your persona. But the narrower your sense of Now, the more tenuous you are."

Because this book is about time and not the larger social issues of surveillance or personality that attend digitalized profusion, we will attend to the time pressures and the time renewals possible and leave those questions alone. Surely digital overload is a key part of the time famine. It is a subset of

Mammon, and that is the larger issue within which our bandwidth problems occur. It's not that they don't matter. Instead we don't have time for them here.

People like us, who have our faces in our phones, may join Walt Whitman in singing the body electric or laugh that the operators of free Wi-Fi kiosks in New York City had to disable their browsing capabilities because men were enjoying free pornography outside. We may be amused and bemused at how much we love to be online like everyone else is. We may wonder how we became such conformists. We may even secretly—or not so secretly—love the Internet. I know part of me does: infatuated with its miraculous, magical qualities.

Virginia Heffernan in *Magic and Loss: The Internet as Art* argues that "the internet is the great masterpiece of human civilization." It is its magical quality that interests her most: "It turns experiences from the material world that used to be densely physical . . . into frictionless, weightless and fantastic abstractions." She closes her book imagining the "mysterious and maddening internet throwing off like a meteor shower a measure of amazing grace." How do we plow our way through the time famine that is caused by the splendor and the excesses of the Internet and its constant cry for communication? How do we live in two spaces, the material and the virtual, at once? These are questions deeply embedded in the time scarcity so many of us feel. I won't be able to answer them, but I will try.

THE ELUSIVENESS OF THE ELEMENTS

I was having a tiresome conversation with a rising second grader (my grandson) about the four elements. He told me they were earth, air, fire, and ice. I told him that they were earth, air, fire, and water, and that ice is a derivative of water. He patronized me about how awful it was that I had been educated in the Pleistocene period. Clearly the four elements were earth, air, fire, and ice. He even hauled out the new Disney movie called *Frozen* and added its importance to his well-armored evidence. He already loves "screen time" more than he does real time—although he does love them both. Just not equally.

I changed the subject, suggesting that the more important question was about the meaning of the word *elemental*, not how many elements there were. I told him that the kind of school he goes to used to be called *elementary school*, a wonderful way of describing the basic and foundational nature of children's education. I tried to get an audience for the three *R*s, but that was way too large an ask, given my audience. I told him the word *elemental* was like the word *fundamental*, that it means what is really important, like the four elements. Then I sprung my developmentally appropriate question:

"What is most important about fire?" He knew right away, having missed the course in modesty early on: "It's knowing how to start a fire and how to put one out." I think he's right. When it comes to digital communication and connection, the fire is raging. We need to know when to turn on and when to turn off our devices. We need to be their master and not their slave. We need to know how to light a fire and how to put one out.

I was once at a summer event of the Good Work Institute, a group of spiritual entrepreneurs who are trying to learn how to do business that regenerates the planet and themselves rather than depleting it. One of the men runs a wilderness camp for children. He takes children, boys especially, into the woods for weekends and teaches them how to light fires and how to tend fires. These rites of passage make a big difference, especially for boys who have no adult male parent. He came to speak to a dozen of our Sunday school parents on a Friday night. He knows how to rub two sticks together to make a fire. It takes about two hours, usually, to get the spark. I used to know how to do this as a girl, but I was astonished at how much I had forgotten. When I got my first spark, along with what can only be called plantar fasciitis of the wrist, I discovered I had forgotten to put dry leaves near me, so I just wasted my spark. "Elementary, my dear Watson," we used to say. Elementary. What bothers me about the disassociation from material space and the move into virtual space—where life becomes a screen—is how it removes us from the physical elements.

As I write this, we just observed the sixteenth anniversary of what is now reduced to the conglomeration of tragedies, experiences, heroism, and long-lasting impact called 9/11. We now have more than one fire to put out, not to mention more than one to light. I guess many of us would like to know how to put out the fire. We wish we had time to put out the fire. We wish we could get free of our tables and chairs and screen time long enough to think our way to preventing the next disaster, and most of us are not elemental enough or educated enough or internally free of brain and soul enough to try. We live knowing that we are not trying to prevent what seems to be a third new reality of natural disasters joining virtual and real disasters. We have what I see as crisis fatigue as well as compassion fatigue. We know that we face interacting disasters, even catastrophes. Public violence joins the major event of 9/11, which joins climate change, which joins Black Lives Matter to create a web of fear and real danger. Because we are already living two lives, the physical and the virtual, we also live in a third world, the one where we are not preparing for an end to violence but an increase in it. We need to prepare, to be proactive about how our already short bandwidth can handle more. That will surely mean deleting more than one file and saying no to more than one presentation by Mammon.

As I was writing this chapter, we woke up on Sunday to news of a pipe bomb in Chelsea. We woke up the following Wednesday to news of a police shooting in Charlotte. And on Saturday we woke up to news of a shooting near Seattle. We are aware that somebody should do something about the trouble we are facing; we just can't imagine that it is us. But we also know that it *has* to be us. The time famine robs us of priority while at the same making us increasingly anxious about our personal safety.

Our parting greeting has changed. We used to say "Have a good day" or "Ta-ta" or, like Winnie the Pooh's friend Tigger, "TTFN"—ta-ta for now. Now we say "Be safe." We consider this a blessing when it is really a disguised curse. Be safe? When I don't know how so to do? When I am aware that the circumstances of safety are beyond my control? And why are they out of my control? I give the answer that I don't have the bandwidth. And I don't.

The fire of 9/11 still burns. On August 22, 2016, at John F. Kennedy International Airport, there was a panic. Someone said there was a live shooter somewhere, and people went nuts, yelling, "Where is he?" As it turned out, there was no shooter. Cops with guns appeared from everywhere. Agents of the Transportation Security Agency fled and hid. It was clear, as they admitted later, that they had no idea what to do. Mostly people just got on their cell phones and tried to find their loved ones until the panic had ended.

You could argue that our movement into virtual reality is a response to increasing public violence: We want to connect with each other and know what is happening. But where is the connection beyond our intimates, the one that will stop interreligious and interracial and intertribal violence? Where is the connection to the physicality of the earth and its elements that will keep us from destroying the planet?

"The [Kennedy] incident proved to me that people working at the airport had no training or plan for responding to such a predictable crisis," wrote a commenter in *New York* magazine later that month. We are so accustomed to terror that we can terrorize ourselves. There are also new technological styles: "This is the baseball cap with an inconspicuous camera that records high definition video," available exclusively from Hammacher Schlemmer. These are astonishing uses of technology, designed to make us safe, but that baseball cap actually scares me to death.

Our Sunday school has had trainings about what to do in the event of an intruder. I remember feeling depressed for two days after those trainings; I just never thought I'd see that day. I also suspect that most people would be so engrossed in their cell phones—even the Sunday school kids—that if something were to happen, the minutes we'd need to save each other would already be lost to the screen.

I personally think that our addiction to our cell phones is a result of 9/11. I've asked people why they are so connected to their cell phones, and they often answer, "Because if something happens, I want to be able to call someone." I do understand. There is a kind of ghost safety in being able to call, and what does it really mean but that we want to not be alone in the universe, to be able to connect to someone? That connection is fundamental and elemental to us. It means everything to us. That's the fire we want to light: the fire of connection, and not just with our intimates. We want that connection with the World Wide Web of people, but we do not make time for that connection because we don't know how. Were the world to become free—or even simply freer than it is—of the constant threat of violent interruption to daily life, we would find ourselves not so anxious about time. We'd have time, instead of time having us.

I am not going to argue that solving the whole fat mess is up to any one of us. It is not. Instead my argument is that the time famine is exacerbated by our sense of powerlessness and by the way we use our phones to placate that feeling. We think that little connection will help appease the loss of big connections across race, class, and religion. A little connection, multiplied, will light the fires of larger more beautiful connection, but first we have to understand the nested meanings of our compulsion to connect. We need direction and time above the physical and the virtual in that gorgeous place called the imagination. That is the place where we will dedicate ourselves to larger connection.

My grandson is also right. We need to learn how to put out fires, and how to light them. We need to devote time to both. We needed to put out the fire yesterday. Environmentalists say we needed to plant the tree yesterday. But since we didn't put out the fire yesterday, instead allowing it to burn, we have bigger fires to put out today and tomorrow.

During this period of the 500th year of the Protestant Reformation, we planned a special service. We wanted to put some fires out. We were not memorializing those great 500 years but rather getting ready to celebrate the beginning of the 501st year or the first year of the *next* reformation. In that year we are going to begin to put out the fire of interreligious hate. The fires of hate that are burning between the religions is out of control—in Israel/Palestine and in the havoc it is reaping in the Black Lives Movement; in terrorism and ISIS and ghost panics and real panics; in the heresies of Christianity across the globe trying to make Jesus number one (as though Jesus wanted that). We need to learn how to put these fires out. These religious fires and religious imperialisms are at the bottom of the trouble that shows up in our watch and on our screen. How did it get so late? We ask ourselves that question almost every couple of hours.

I say this as a religious person, one who loves religion but also hates what it tries to do in the name of the God, beyond God. We may not think we have time to be religious or truly spiritual, or to start or put out fires. We actually have time only for that; otherwise it will be too late.

The elemental use of time is to learn how to spark a new religion, a new peace that will be within us and beyond us. But then there is the normal life of tending and keeping oneself together. We got back from our summer place this week only to find that someone had put anchovies in the dryer. All the dry towels smelled like anchovies, the dryer smelled like anchovies, and, as absurd and unlikely as it may seem, someone *definitely* put anchovies in the dryer. I know this is absurd—and things like this happen to all of us and prevent us from fundamentals or elementals or sparking a new religion. I relate this experience just to give context to how absurd it is that *religions* are the source of fires that we don't know how to put out. Just take that in. Religious discord is destroying the world. It is like that folk saying about the cobbler's children having no shoes. I want religion to have impact, but one that doesn't shout and one that doesn't shoot. But I am also worried about making the 8:18 train to work and figuring out how to order a new dryer. I know you are too. Living virtually and physically—in a world in great danger—is such a recipe for an ongoing time famine that I barely know where to start.

The place to start is in confronting how overwhelmed we are in elemental and elementary ways, not in going numb or staying in denial about the trouble. That is what we really don't have time for. It won't help get us to the place of genuine understanding of what is important. What is important is to stop the hate and start the love, to trust each other and to connect with each other, with or without cell phones. What matters is our inner peace and our outer peace. Peace is very different from safety. Connection to our intimates and to strangers is very different from knowing what table somebody is hiding under at the airport during a bomb scare. Peace is what true religion actually promises. That is the fire—the fire of peace—that we need to start.

RUBBING TWO TWIGS TOGETHER TO GET A SPARK

There is no reason to be overwhelmed about peace. It is actually a gift, not a get. Because the creator has given you the gift of peace—however you name him, her, it, or them—you don't need to fret about not having it. It is already yours. The anxiety and fear about not having it creates the time famine and the roaring, raging fires between us.

I like to think of my life as collecting twigs, and knowing when to put those twigs into life and let them touch each other. You never know which member of the community is going to spark you. You also know you need to keep the fires small. And if you want to find a spark, look in the ashes. Stare straight at the ashes of 9/11 and you may find yourself inspired to twig and spark a fire. In our sparking we can also imitate nature, physically. The duration of the existence of a spark is determined by the initial size of the particle, with a larger size leading to a longer-lasting spark.

I want you all to be collectors of twigs and creators of sparks. I want you to know how to tend fires—which means putting some out and starting some elsewhere. I want you to know how to rub sticks together to get friction and how to be a part of community. I want you to be keepers and collectors. Yes, I mean these things metaphorically and spiritually. There is plenty of time to collect a few twigs and to light a few sparks. It is actually elemental work, and it can be done even if people put anchovies in your dryer. How? By paying attention to what is important and then attending to the physical and virtual world. A friend who recently died used to always ask the same question of everyone: "How is your spiritual condition?" That is the question we constantly ask of ourselves and others when we go elemental.

Let's pay a little attention to that word *keep* and that word *collect*. You need to collect twigs to start a fire. You need to keep a fire going by tending it. Lots of people collect things that they then tend. In fact, collecting is a habit many of us have to bide away our time. More often than not, we collect for recreational purposes. Collecting is like connecting: We keep things around us. There is nothing elemental about having a collection of something, but having a collection shows a kind of peace in living. It shows that you have extra time, time you use recreationally. You stop being the kind of person who says, "My house is a mess" and become a person who says, "I have a collection. Do you want to see it?"

There was a show called *The Keeper* at the New Museum in New York City, which exhibited a series of collections. The whole show featured more than two dozen collectors and more than four thousand objects, including a collection of teddy bears, street trash, rare rocks, butterflies, photos of snowflakes, and Zofia Rydet's "Sociological Record," a project in which she photographed the interior of nearly twenty thousand homes in Poland. The people who are keepers are considered an artistic meditation on values. Each collection is "an activity that exposes, even as it deflects, our fears that the universe couldn't care less about our hankering selves," as the *New Yorker* puts its summary ("The Keeper"). When we live in the time famine, we double-time ourselves, virtually or physically. Why do we do this? Because we think the universe doesn't care about us. But, oddly and beautifully, it does. We don't even need all that stuff to prove or improve our existence; instead, it is just fun to have it. People who go elemental about, let's say, world peace or inner peace also have time to play. That may sound odd, but it's not. We both pray and play with purpose. We start with knowing that peace is a gift and that we no longer have to work for it or at it. That graceful experience of peace turns our behavior into peace. In peace, we have hope to put out the raging fires and start the twinkling ones. In peace, we have time to play as well.

The act of keeping, these artists argue, is one of self-preservation. I know this is true. My mother's Boyds teddy bear collection grounds her. She is proud that she has 248 bears, and cannot pass a yard sale or a thrift store without looking for another one. My husband has more than 200 snow globes, representing most states and cities in the United States and a large number of places in Europe, too. (My favorite is his Mormon Tabernacle snow globe.) Why do we collect things? Why not? There are deeper reasons for collecting that attend to the time famine. We want others to connect with us, and we want to connect to them. We collect to show people that we are here, cell phones and all. We collect to identify ourselves and to display our uniqueness. That quest to express what is unique about us also springs from the great gift of peace: We want to show God and the world what our spiritual DNA involves.

Erin Thompson writes:

> The oil billionaire J. Paul Getty was famously miserly. He installed a pay-phone in his mansion in Surrey, England, to stop visitors from making long-distance calls. He refused to pay ransom for a kidnapped grandson for so long that the frustrated kidnappers sent Getty his grandson's ear in the mail. Yet he spent millions of dollars on art, and millions more to build the Getty Museum in Los Angeles. He called himself "an apparently incurable art-collecting addict," and noted that he had vowed to stop collecting several times, only to suffer "massive relapses." Fearful of airplanes and too busy to take the time to sail to California from his adopted hometown of London, he never even visited the museum his money had filled. ("Why People Collect Art")

Imagine not having time to become yourself or to receive the gift of peace. Imagine being an accidental artist, one who never got to enjoy his collection. Imagine being so lacking in peace that you couldn't even give away a little of all the money that you have to save a grandson. That is not wealth; it is poverty.

Wealth is having enough time to imagine a beautiful world for everyone while having one yourself. Wealth is the opposite of famine. It is the blissful state of having enough. It is the peaceful pursuit of small projects, like having a collection, and nesting in the larger project of God's great gift of life to us all.

THE ART OF SPIRITUAL TINKERING

At my congregation, we have long been about the art of spiritual tinkering or spiritual experimentation. It's just who we are. It's just the way we are, as one of our mothers argued the other night. When her son would ask, "Why do I have to visit the old woman down the hall?" her answer was: "That's who we are." Another parent said that we here at Judson enjoy spirited service—which is collecting twigs to spark fire for each other. When we do something meaningful and self-disclosing, when we collect things that matter, we find ourselves building fires, not putting them out. We go positive in a world that is crazy negative. We get a little above and ahead of physical time and virtual time. We enjoy time. We are in time. We are in time with others. That is the point of it all anyway—and that is what peace gives us.

I am adopting the nickname Rip Van Twinkle. I feel like I was born either too late or too early; I can tell by the way people stare at my notebooks and cardboard calendars. But the truth is, I was born when I was born and will die when I die. My collections will not come with me, but they will alert people that a person like me—who has no collections, only a twig box—was around. When we find ourselves stressed—virtually or physically or by the latest catastrophe—the best antidote is to move into our time, our way, taking our stuff and our identity with us. Why live for someone else, or in someone else's way—even your grandson's? We can imitate Rip Van Winkle in being astonished that there are kids around who think ice is an element because Disney said so, or instead we can be people who stood in that first year of what's new and next and saw it and loved it up. We can live in our time our ways, in our days our ways, collecting whatever pleases us.

If we'd built a good fire, how would we know? The kids would hate to leave school; we'd have to make them leave. Religion would stop being the source of war and become a fountain of peace. People would have astonishing collections and believe their presence on the planet mattered. If you didn't get to all your e-mails yesterday, or today, you wouldn't fret. You'd be much more interested in real connection than in obligated connection. The cobbler's children would have shoes. We would all be connected to what is elemental. And we'd be sparks for each other's warmth and fire.

As Bishop Yvette Flunder has said over and over: Hurt people hurt people. They have been burned. Healed people heal people. They know how to tend fires and keep fires and spark fires. They know how to warm people and not burn them.

STEWARDSHIP AS TENDING AND NEGOTIATING

Starting and stopping fires is important. So is making a deal with the universe about how big your own personal fire ought to be or not be. There is a delightfully complex text about stewardship in Luke 16, often called the Parable of the Shrewd Steward. It goes into the intricacies of debt and tending, both of which are a part of getting your own personal fire to the right size. Neither you nor I alone is in charge of world peace. We are charged by our great thanksgiving to be part of a great peace. The divine accepts partial payments.

In the parable, the steward has disappointed his master, who wants to know why the steward was not out collecting payments. He feels cheated.

The steward is afraid that he will be put out and have nowhere to go, so he shrewdly tells the master's debtors that they can make partial payment. You owe the master one thousand jars of olive oil? Pay him eight hundred. You owe the master seventy shares of wheat? Pay him forty. The master thanks the steward for being honest, after having been dishonest, for being accountable, after having been unaccountable, and brings him back into his good graces. In the story the master is not God, as so often is the case in the parables of Jesus. The master himself is a steward of God's gifts.

Many say that the steward and the master are in the story to prove a point: None of this belongs to us, anyway; it is all a loan. We are here to tend our loans. That is what is elemental.

When we move from a position of ownership to a position of receivership, when we reimagine ourselves as stewards instead of owners, peace is the consequence. We have only the job of tending, not owning. Instead of walking around with the stooped shoulders of "It's all up to us," we have the freed shoulders of "Thank you, God, for your trust in us." We have only the job of being honest stewards.

A collect is an old-fashioned, one-sentence prayer that integrates the appointed lessons for the day, using the psalm as a key to open the other three. In most Christian traditions, preachers are taught to write collects and to read the entire "periscope" or group of weekly texts together. The appointed day for this parable from Luke includes three other richly connected texts. I like to collect scriptural texts. I like to write collects too.

In this story of a steward who is in trouble with his master, we have joined to it, in the liturgy, an admonition from the Epistles to pray even for the kings, that they may rightly steward their power, and a scathing attack on the rich from Amos that God will not forget those who "throw the poor into the dust and trash them in the dung pile." (That is the King James Version, usually the one with a little more elegant language.) The psalm insists that we are to spend our days in praise, not work.

Stewardship, spiritually and materially, feels like work, accountability, accounts, and accounting. It feels the way many of us do many days, needing to do more and be more than we are capable of doing or being. Surely the master is involved in an accounting with his steward and the steward is involved in accounting with his master. The steward then goes on to a shrewd recounting with the master's debtors and allows sagacity to win the day. They pay a margin of what they owe, and the master is happy to get it. In one sentence, one might say the theme is "Do what you can with what you have." That would be honest instead of dishonest wealth. That would also combine the stewardship of tending to the stewardship of negotiating. In negotiation, you do what you can with what you have.

One might also say that Amos was telling a fib when he said God would not forget those who oppress the poor and sell them down the river for a shoe. God is willing to negotiate, just as the master was willing to accept less than perfection.

We all know that we are to be good stewards. Only the truly conceited among us think that we earn what we have. I know the story of a used-car dealer who swore he was a self-made man, even though he inherited the dealership from his father. But most of us know our debt to the divine, our credit card debt with the creator, our accounts payable ledger and the last time it was prayerfully audited.

We may know that we are to be good stewards, but we rarely find ways so to be. We connive. We take the potluck dish and its ingredients off our tithe when we go to the church or school supper. We inflate our carefulness and deflate our carelessness. How else could we go to sleep at night? We know that we are to spend our days in praise instead of in traffic. We know that we are to spend our days in praise of God and to work as though we don't really need the money. But instead we collect stars on our report cards and attend our résumés, all with a kind of grudge. So many of us, deep down, have the sneaking suspicion that it's all up to us. I know I think that, and not just when I am tired or weary with well doing. Like most people I know, I have a great fear that I'm really not okay, that God's grace applies to other people and not to me. I don't know who convinced so many of us of our unworthiness. They surely were not good stewards. They surely did not spend their days in praise. They surely were not elemental or well schooled in elementary matters. And they certainly don't know how hard most of us work just to keep our heads above water, much less worship God while attending Mammon. We try not to double-time the divine—and yet most of us do just that.

The Luke story ends with what feels like a preachy add-on: "You cannot worship both God and Money." But why can't we, as long as one is more important to us than the other? Sure, we are to worship God and not Mammon's accounts. But doesn't the master in this tale like the steward's fix? And what is all that stuff about heavenly rewards after we've been talking about wheat and tares? I don't get the switch to the spiritual when we have been so delightfully fixated on the material. The material *is* important. The spiritual *is* important. We live in a world of both God and Mammon. We worship one and tend the other; we praise one and negotiate with the other. Neither activity is better than the other. We are creatures, not owners, of the universe.

I remember a confirmand of mine once responded to a church fight about someone's sexual orientation: "Thank God they're finally talking about something that matters." Matter and materiality matter to people. They are the platform on which we dance our virtue. We make real choices in real time about God and about Mammon. Less of Mammon makes space for more of God. We make the choice to talk about something that really matters.

Getty gave a great gift to the universe, one he never learned how to enjoy. According to Thompson, "His most important investment was in the identity-granting power of art." It helped him feel good about himself. Collecting money and collecting debts and being material makes us feel good. We like wealth, and lots of it—and we also want to figure out how to enjoy honest wealth, one not at the expense of the poor or the enslaved or the other merchants with whom we work, or even the king. We expect the king to use power well, and we hope we ourselves will do the same thing.

We start fires. We stop fires. We tend fires. We negotiate the size of our fires and their beauty. That is what is important. And it all starts with knowing we are gifted creatures of a great God. It also stops there. Creatures don't hurt each other. Creatures help each other. Creatures tend each other. Creatures spend their lives in praise, not in power grabs.

As long as praise, thanksgiving, and creature knowledge top our daily to-do and to-be list, we will no longer have to fret about the virtual world or the material world. They will have found their appropriate home in a larger stewardship of great gifts. We will peacefully double or triple our time in multiple worlds. That is elementary and elemental.

O God, you so worthy of praise, keep our foot off the backs of the poor, our hearts in respect for all, especially the honest kings and rich merchants who use their power well, and let us be savvy, always, when in the presence of money. Amen.

Chapter Six

Doing Something New

It is amazing how long people as smart as you and I are will keep doing the same thing over and over again, as though it were working. We give the word *rut* and the idea of the hamster wheel new meaning all the time. And why not? Rut could also mean pattern. It could even mean spiritual practice. Let's not dismiss rut prematurely as a negative, but figure out how to determine what is a rut and what is a practice. It has to do with intention.

When I finally learned to circle my garden, it stopped driving me crazy. It was driving me crazy because I could never get it "just right." I could never get the weeding done. So I learned to tend and befriend its unfinished imperfection. I learned how to turn my garden into something I could love. I removed it from the category of obligation into the category of gift. Spiritual boldness comes from knowing you are loved and that therefore you can love. Love is a place beyond obligation. You learn to circle and cycle instead of fussing and fretting. You circle instead of marching forward to some unachievable goal. Since you start with peace, you can end with peace as well.

CIRCLING THE GARDEN

I learned a new way of gardening once the old ways collapsed within me. I had a three-acre farm in downtown Amherst, Massachusetts. There were ten separate gardens to tend, the biggest one for vegetables and nine smaller ones for an inheritance of rare and interesting perennials. I nearly killed myself keeping up with the work. Then I tried something new: Each day of good gardening weather, I would tend one garden. On the weekends I would tame the vegetable garden. Instead of the heeding the gardens' all yelling at me all the time—Tend me! Weed me! Touch me!—I would let them be. It's not your day yet, I would counsel them. I learned how to clean my house in this circling way too. The point is less a hint from Heloise than it is a time-management system: I will do what I can with what I have; I won't do more than I can. Some dust bunnies and some weeds will have to wait. I am in charge of my time. My obligations are not in charge of my time.

WHY DON'T WE TRY SOMETHING NEW?

The reason for our lack of spiritual boldness has to do with how excruciating it is to be wrong and to know you are wrong. Many of us just don't believe we are or were really loved. We can't fathom a God who loves us unconditionally. The reasons are generational and deep. Our parents probably didn't know unconditionality either. That was someplace we were supposed to go, not a place we were given.

When I was allowing that magnificent garden to corner and circle me, I did not have a good sense of time. I was out of time all the time. I was not just lacking time; I was out of time, while being in time, wasting my time.

Being Wrong: Adventures in the Margin of Error is a magnificent book, recommended by the president of Harvard as one she wishes all students would read. In it, Kathryn Schulz describes doubt as the fountain of wisdom. Why would we not have doubts about the way we live? Instead of loving rare perennials, we worry that we are not weeding them adequately. People don't have time to take care of their children or their parents, outsourcing this work and paying others to do it. Why don't we have enough time? Because we are very busy being successful on somebody else's terms. In the Parable of the Great Banquet, with its eloquent slave who had to tell the master bad news, Jesus suggests that we learn to be unsuccessful and proud of it. In the movie *Moneyball*, the message is similar: "If you change what is meant by winning, you change the game" and "We value players that other people don't." The gospel takes what you think life is—getting a good seat at a good price, rushing, working, pleasing, doing what the master tells you to do—and tells you that is not life. Life is everybody at the table. The gospel always puts a different paint job on what we think reality is. Even a little bit of trust in the alternative narrative allows us to enjoy doubt and to try something new. Even a little bit of inner peace allows us to worship God and money, in the right balance. None of us is ever going to get the balance right. I personally am an avid imperfectionist. People when the Bible was being written and gathered didn't get it right, and neither will we. That being said, aiming to worship God will both make for inner peace and be the result of inner peace. We will be doing what is primary in a primary way, what is first in a first way.

My good friend James Forbes says that the difference between black and white churches is that white churches think God needs them and black churches think they need God. One is a host and the other is a guest. One has worship committees and the other worships. One thinks of itself as very good; the other is less sure. One puts God first and the other puts their own Mammon first.

My own route to God's grace and to the table has been through my weakness, not my strength. Most people finally figure out, with Edith Hamilton, "that the fullness of life is in the hazards of life." We need trouble to make us well. We need trouble to discover that God really loves us.

Because of the largest crisis in my relatively untroubled life, I became a guest and stopped hosting for a while. I survived breast cancer fifteen years ago. When I had my mastectomy, I knew I needed God. I was carried by prayer through the whole thing—and not by reminding people that they needed to add care for me to their list of duties. I learned to trust the team around me. I was carried by others who loved me. It was the best thing that ever happened to my competence. I stopped carrying for a while and let myself be carried. I also have watched the failure, so far, of my life's work in ending racism and poverty. I have learned to be someone in need as well as someone who has something to give. I have learned that I don't know everything, even though I am a part of a smart, caring, and giving church. People get spiritual indigestion in a world where we are always the helper and others are being helped; learning to be carried is spiritual Alka-Seltzer.

When we prepare to do something new, the first stop on our way is being wrong and knowing we are wrong. The second stop is doubting the rightness of what we are doing. The third stop is diving deep to find out why we wrong ourselves with the time famine. After we unlearn the stuff that is actually hurting—even killing—us, we are ready to circle and cycle. We jump off the treadmill. We get out of our ruts.

There is a deep-down consensus among Americans, on both sides of the aisle, that "it's all about the money." I wonder what would happen if we actually faced the absurd role money now has in our politics, our government, our own lives. I wonder what would happen if we said to each other, "I am powerless over money and the grab it has on my life and the life of the poor and the life of my church." Note echoes of the Alcoholics Anonymous rhythm there: "We are powerless over alcohol and its grip on our lives," say people in AA. What about saying we are powerless over money, too, out loud and in a group? Doesn't our money driver like to take us to places we don't really want to go?

Let me give a second, more systemic example. With regard to immigration, we puff ourselves up and act as though we are the hosts and immigrants are the guests. They are a permanent *they*, who only take and do not give. When people are allowed to say, "I bought twenty-four pairs of legs today"—meaning "I hired twelve immigrants"—we are in great danger as a nation. We have objectified human beings. Immigrants are deserving of America. I am also deserving of America. You are, too. There is no *we* and no *they*. There is no one who doesn't deserve a place at the table. Those who want a nation of only one color or one food or one race are fossilizing as hosts. Nobody will accept the invitation to that party, because it's not a party, but instead a control feast. Why do we hurt and insult immigrants? Because we doubt and mistrust our own ways and our own days. And because we are afraid of losing money to them. We do strange things and hurtful things because we can't risk a new way.

The time famine comes from internalized capitalism. We've simply been doing what "everybody" does, valuing what "everybody" values. This conformity is our spiritual rut. Instead of self-blame, forgiveness is a good place to start. You may forgive yourself for internalizing capitalism. This spiritual repentance becomes a permission (out of which grows an internalized commitment) to enter our difficulty with hope and conviction, not with shame or blame.

Storytelling is the essential and important first step. Tell your story of money, power, and debt. Tell your story of repentance, too. Were you so ashamed about losing your job that you didn't tell anybody? Who are your people, and what is the story of your people's journey through the lands of money, power, and debt? Do you have student debt? Do you have despair about what it bought you or can buy you? Are you underwater in your mortgage? Have you found a way out of shame about not being rich in a land where gaining wealth is the eleventh commandment? Do you allow yourself to be driven by money, while accusing other people of doing the same?

Tell your story whenever, wherever, and however you can. Engage the people around you. Listen to their story. Think of NPR's popular StoryCorps and you will see where this is going. We can imagine a great consciousness-raising experience, where aha moments go viral. "I thought I was the only one in this congregation with crushing debt." *Aha! I am not.* "I thought I was the only person who thought I was bad for not being successful." *Aha! I am not.* "I thought I was the only person who knew that the system was rigged and that money in politics had destroyed the American dream and the dreamers." *Aha! I am not.*

The second step is to learn some new mantras. I like these. I pray them or sing them aloud to myself. They help, especially if I know some of my friends have heard my story of being driven by money.

> This is my vow: To live content with small means, to seek elegance rather than luxury, and refinement rather than fashion, to be worthy not respectable, to be wealthy, not rich, to think quietly, talk gently, act frankly, to listen to stars and sages, babes and birds, and to do all bravely, to await occasion, hurry never . . . in a world, to let the spiritual, unbidden and unconscious, grow up through the common. Let this be my symphony.
> —Adapted from the Credo of William Ellery Channing

I vow again to live alert to the rich deep murmur of the past. I vow to find the comfort in what has been. I vow to be unafraid of change, insatiable in intellectual curiosity, interested in big things, and happy in small ways.
—Adapted from Edith Wharton

Now is the time to know that all you do is sacred. Why not consider a lasting truce with yourself and God? All your ideas of right and wrong were just a child's training wheels to be laid aside so you can finally live with veracity and love. Please tell me: why do you throw sticks at your heart inside? They only incite you to fear. Now is the time for the world to know that everything, thought and action alike, is sacred. Deeply compute the possibility that there is anything but grace.
—Hafiz, from "The Gift"

I know rags and I know riches; each has a beauty when it is not afraid of the other. Grace lives where you need nothing; obligation lives where you need everything. Money likes to turn us into people who are so wrong that we wrong others; remember: Hurt people hurt people; healed people heal people. Doing something new is healing ourselves and then letting the stories flow out of us toward others. Before we can do something new, we need inner healing around our own doubleness.

SWITCHING THE CHANNEL IN
OUR BRAINS AND SOULS

Doing something new is the opposite of being in a rut. Doing something new is sometimes as simple as switching the channel. I have spent way too much of my life listening to the channel that said I wasn't enough if I didn't have enough money to take care of myself and to "look good." But when I switch the channel, I often hear the most beautiful and unusual music.

Deep in one March Madness season, I was in the airport. There a big crowd was snow delayed for somewhere or another. I really wanted to watch the Stanford women's game instead of the Duke men's game. I whispered a request to one man, who sent it to another—and next thing I knew, the channel had switched and we were watching the women play. I took ridiculous joy in this small victory—and I have had even more joy in larger switches of larger channels.

I have nothing against men's basketball, or, for that matter, men. I could even tell you about some of the men I have really enjoyed. But what I know about my life is that I was always switching the channel. Most people think male clergy are too feminine and female clergy are too masculine. Isn't that wonderful? I am so grateful to have worked in a place that doesn't know how to be a gender role prison, and to have a daughter who is queer, in the way I still hope to be. Queer people have as their primary enemy the false binary.

They think we can be a little of both or a lot of both. They resist gender boxes, and that resistance, all by itself, creates space and time. It also gives Mammon a hard time.

The biggest problem for my security might have been success, wealth, and status. Instead it was self-righteousness. I often wondered why others couldn't find their way. My biggest problem in writing this book is to answer to myself the question: Who cares? A second problem is to keep it from a sneaky brag instead of a sincere thanks. Carl Jung says we sneak our biography into everything we say. I think this is true, so I'm sure I won't avoid the bragging. I am proud. I also know how violent it has been for me and to me to think of my grace and salvation as having been earned.

There is a parallel trap in the way we treat the poor: Is their poverty their fault? Shouldn't they just work harder? Likewise parents whose children aren't successful, whatever that means: Isn't it their fault? Can they also take the credit, if things go well for their children?

Religious self-righteousness is particularly galling; it is actually the main reason so many of us are religiously allergic. Truly sheltered people peek around the corner of shelter and abundance, job and role, income and security, to a larger and stronger foundation. We believe both that we deserve goodness and that we haven't earned it. We aren't what we do; we are what we are. We are the gifted, who know that we are gifted. I do not mean talented, but gifted; there is a difference. We have the spiritual right and capacity to trust ourselves. That trust helps us trust others, wherever they are on their journey. We know only one way home. We don't know all the ways home. We do protect and tend one story about what it means to be a human being, and it is our spiritual home.

What is really new is conquering the time famine and *not* becoming self-righteous about it. There is a trick to accepting a gift: saying thank-you, without secretly thinking you deserved it. Self-righteousness is the one thing the divine really dislikes.

In the amazement of grace, we figure out that we love rags *and* riches; or, better put, that we love something like life more than either rags or riches. We don't live to avoid rags or to get riches. We live differently. We live "contented with small means." Money no longer tells us who we are. I have a lovely, if shabby, wardrobe and haven't bought outside of a thrift store or a yard sale for years. When people "roast" me at awards ceremonies and farewells, they comment on how good my style and my wardrobe are. My favorite activity is to go book shopping at the Amherst town dump's free bookstore. There I also like to pick up some mulch for the garden, and just about whatever else is laying around.

Am I bragging or confessing? The truth is, I am doing both. I am bragging because I have taken a lot of money and turned it into even more. Ever since I cashed my first factory paycheck, I have just loved having money in my pocket. I don't particularly like spending it; I just like having it there. It may be that I too want the security of that $500 escape money I gave my mother—the first money I ever made as a minister—to use to run off if he ever hit her again. It wasn't generosity on my part. Until she was safer, I couldn't spend money on anything else. That was then. Now I have changed and spent serious money on a country place so I could garden, even while working in New York City. I have given myself permission to have a spiritual home, even though I am richly aware of how homeless so many are, in so many different ways. I don't deserve my wealth. Others don't deserve their poverty. These matters both lie in that land beyond the cliché that we are all in it for the money. We are not in it for the money. We are in it because God gave us the gift of life.

HOW WILL YOU KNOW IF YOU'RE OUT OF THE RUT AND INTO THE PRACTICE?

I preach a lot of sermons. One day in a review course I had taken on preaching, I realized that the methods for writing a sermon are the same methods we use in assessing a life.

The old-fashioned way to preach a sermon was a one-line exegesis of the text and three points, a repeat of the one liner, and an amen, within twenty or so minutes. You look for a good central image and just work it over and over. My associate Micah Bucey once preached a great sermon about his grandmother's chocolate cake recipe. On the old, tattered recipe, she had written, "Take care of this." One way to evaluate a life is to figure out what you have taken care of. He was preaching on that interesting text from Luke 13 on God and Mammon and about how the shrewd steward actually knew how to take care of business.

I wrote in the first chapter that the roots of the time famine are in this double-timing of God and Mammon. Here I want to show how to shrewdly live beyond that doubleness and into a practical flow from one to the other, where the God part automatically leads the money part. We aren't anti-money so much as pro-God.

Think of it this way: There was a sign in a church that said, "God Is Other People." Someone inserted a comma: "God Is Other, People." There is nothing wrong with people so much as getting them to be your God. There is nothing wrong with Mammon except letting it become your God.

There are lots of ways to preach and lots of ways to live. Professor Fred Craddock advises us to be intuitive. The shrewd steward text often leaves people confused, because the first half of it is about the virtue in compromise and the second half says there is no compromise. God and money cannot both be served. (There are other texts where this shows up: Matthew 6:24 and also Exodus 20, on the golden calf. But this text gives a complex rationale about God and money.)

The second half of the text sets the basic frame: You can't do both God and Mammon. The first half of Luke 13 is all messed up, because the shrewd steward is indeed apparently serving God and Mammon quite well. Intuitively and rationally, we are confused by this text. A lot of lives remain as confused as many sermons.

Professor Edmund Steimle advises that we just stick with the story. This we can do with this text, because it is a great story. The master upbraids his employee, the steward. The steward gets upset. He thinks he is out of a job. "I can neither dig nor beg," he says. The steward gets crafty. He makes a deal with the master's debtors. They are happy. Then, perplexingly, the master is also happy. If you could get rid of the preachy second half of the text, you could simply say in your one-line exegesis, "God loves a cheerful bargainer." And if you're not interested in preaching or its professors, you could just say that all these approaches apply to a life as well. How do you exegete a life or its passage? You think intuitively. You just tell its story, and this will tell you what kind of rut you have inhabited. Yes, we all live in ruts. We plow the same ground, even if the ground is always trying to become new.

Professor Rick Lowry advises another direction to understanding a text or a life: Follow the plot. What happened to make other things happen? How did the actors manage their interruptions along the way? In the parable, the steward became shrewd: He made a way where there was no way.

Professor Jonathan Mitchell imagines the gospel as celebration and wants every story to show off God in a new and good way. He thinks scripture exists to make God look good. Here we find a hidden God, the one behind the master. This God is arguing that none of this belongs to any of us: Not the oil, not the wheat, not the money, not the exchange. This story is probably a kingdom text or a commonwealth text or a text that tells what it will be like when God is in charge again, as in Creation. There won't be money unevenly exchanged; exchange will be equal. There won't be masters or stewards. In that great waking-up morning, there will be a profound evenness and goodness. Thus the master can applaud compromise over things that don't ultimately matter. That peace deposited in us in the beginning will be the peace at the end. All was well, is well, and will be well. Thank you, Hildegard, who said that all is well, all will be well.

Professor David Buttrick argues that preaching is just a series of moves. Professor Thomas Long argues similarly for attention to the various images and how they turn the story. I usually preach out of their direction and live out of their own intended direction. In the shrewd steward text, a half dozen moves, almost all surprising, show the shrewdness of the steward. Then we move over into the telling part, after the story, where the master pontificates, and does so out of compliance with the lived life of the story. He gets preachy. He says we can't worship God and Mammon, even though the whole story says you can. The story loves compromise; the teaching hates it. Welcome to most of our lives. Becoming new has to do with naming the compromises we have had to make.

A new interpreter in my world is Leah Schade, who wrote *Creation-Crisis Preaching: Ecology, Theology, and the Pulpit.* She says that we should look at texts from the point of view of the animals or the natural objects in the story, like the wheat and the oil. I have many pictures in my head of the hilarious conversation between jars of oil and tares of wheat, all assembled and bottled or bagged in a grocery store at two o'clock in the morning. They come alive and start talking: "They think they own us." "They think they can buy and sell us." "They think we care."

Where you were born, whether you live in a cold or warm climate, what kind of animals are or are not outside your door *matters.* You are a creature in a natured time and place. The rut you are in is determined by temperature as well as climate. You may be in a place where it is easy to get food, so easy to get that you get lots of it whenever you want. That alone causes a time famine, as evidenced by how many people get flustered even about dinner choices. You may live in a world where the whole day is involved in obtaining water or food, which causes another kind of time famine. We are all creatures, no matter where we are from. God thinks of us all the same—not as better or worse than each other.

The master's absurd testimony about not being able to worship God and Mammon just shows what a master he is. He thinks he is in charge of telling people what to think and in charge of what the price is on things that actually have no price. He was doing much better when he accepted his steward's partial payment. He was more godly. God forgives and knows. God created us to be imperfect, not perfect.

I don't mean to be hostile to the master, only to his ways. I need to be able to criticize and I also need criticism. Otherwise I just get happy in my rut and usually join self-righteousness to it.

Without danger or darkness or criticism, we rarely dive deep. The larger point of this text is that we never owned any of this in the first place, thus we are able to be shrewd about the unimportant matters of the so-called cost of wheat and oil, the imaginary time famine and its ways with us. We can actually learn the art of compromise and learn it calmly, without anxiety about ownership or how important our opinions are (if we are masters) or how shrewd our behavior is (if we are slaves or stewards). We can learn to steward our time and take care of it: "Take care of this please."

One of the ruts in which we can live quite nicely is the one where we are not in charge, not perfect, and destined to make mistakes. This is a spiritual practice, without the self-righteousness that usually attaches to a good spiritual practice. We will even make mistakes in how to interpret our lives. We won't preach good sermons all the time. We won't always know exactly what is going on, especially if half of our life is in the crowded virtual world and the other half in the crowded and cluttered material world.

When night and day balance perfectly within you, as they do in the equinox, for example, we find that we are becoming human in a natural way. We change our minds. We make new choices. We de-rut, only to re-rut. We call this spiritual practice.

A few days ago, as I write this, the marriage announcement for Jules Feiffer and JZ Holden appeared in the *New York Times*. He has been married three times; she, twice. They met in a class on writing that he was teaching: "'His class, humor and truth, was enormously challenging. He asked us to take our biggest betrayals and make them funny,' said Ms. Holden, who had written about being abused as a child and of her 1995 divorce. 'At first I was outraged. How dare he? Then I realized how attached I was to my story. That was a big aha moment. How ridiculous it suddenly seemed to have nursed that hurt over so many years.'"

Most of us have been nursing a story over many years. It might be a self-congratulatory story or a guilty one or an injured one. Checking out which story we are telling ourselves about ourselves, with some humor, grace, or peace, would go a long way toward our becoming new. It would de-rut us to re-rut us.

A lot of us have stomachaches about things we think we are supposed to attend. This stomachache comes from thinking we *must* do something. Instead, we *may* do something. We can trust the universe that God already owns. When we get free of the puffed-upness of having to do something, we become free to do something. And we do something—not everything, but something—from a point of compromising virtue. We become shrewd and stop working on being smart. We steward. We take care of things. We know we have debt we cannot pay. We become less afraid of our mistakes and more interested in our next move. Thank you, Professor Buttrick.

The gospel is the good news that we get a next move. The texts are all about who makes the next move. The gospel understands the importance of moving, even after you have been struck down.

Are ownership and its obligations not the foundation of our anxiety? We are supposed to do something. Many of us are desperate to do nothing for a while, so earnest and consequential have we become about all the important things we are doing. It could be that doing less is doing more about the important things, like getting people around the globe to get along. We do less in order to restore our capacity to care about others. We may not save them or help them, but at least we aren't too preoccupied with our mastering selves to even care about them.

My friend Mary is cutting a peach tree down, slowly. It was one she and her now-deceased husband planted together on a beautiful fall afternoon. It's not crazy important, and then again, it actually *is* crazy important. She is doing something useless to honor something that is in her and that was in them. Often useless or open time gives us the capacity to care about something besides ourselves.

If you don't like ordinary examples of ordinary people, then look long and hard at the ego crisis of a certain Mr. J. Paul Getty. Like the master, he thought he had to do things to get people to notice him. He was an accidental giver to the world. His story is a kind of shrewd if sad stewardship.

> Getty is only one of the many people through history who have gone to great lengths to collect art—searching, spending, and even stealing to satisfy their cravings. But what motivates these collectors?
>
> Getty was not even from New York or Boston. He grew up in the scraped-together oil-boom towns of the Great Plains and the brand-new expanses of Los Angeles. But he made his first million by the time he was 24, prospecting for oil in Oklahoma in 1916. He promptly retired, declaring that he would henceforth live a life of enjoyment of beaches and fast cars. But Getty's California idyll proved to bore him, and he began to work again after little more than a year. He did so for the rest of his long life, travelling constantly, sleeping little, trusting few, and accumulating a vast fortune—at $2 billion by the time of his death, thanks to Getty Oil's worldwide network of oil production and distribution.
>
> When Getty started to collect art, his focus on buying Greek and Roman antiquities went against the American zeitgeist. Getty's most important investment was in the identity-granting power of art. (Thompson, "Why People Collect Art")

We expect the masters to use power well and hope we ourselves will do the same thing. Was Getty a child of the light or a child of the darkness? Did he ever really own his art? I wonder.

The text we have been niggling this whole book—and perhaps our whole life—means one big thing. The oil, the wheat, the life never belonged to you in the first place. Once you get there, then you can learn to compromise, shrewdly. You can also worship the God beyond Mammon, the one who spends most of the time stargazing as opposed to counting up your idolatrous points on a great tally sheet.

There is a place between passivity and violence. Passivity is when you are just plain lazy. This laziness comes from deep within the existential sense that you don't matter, that the universe does not care. It comes from the sense that you are small in a small way. Violence is something we do to ourselves when we work too hard or something terrorists or deeply disturbed people do when they have to have things their way. I'd like to meet you there, in that place between passivity and violence. I'd like to meet you where you do what you can with what you have.

This quote is a great rewrite of Rumi: "There is a place beyond virtue. I'll meet you there. It is a compromised place. It is a good place. It worships God and works with Mammon. Passivity is lazy; violence is the result of thinking it's all up to you. I'll meet you there." I can't find the source of this quote, and it is not mine. But it is just very good.

BEYOND THE RUT AND INTO
THE PRACTICE OF IMPERFECTION

You will know you are out of a rut when you have the capacity to care both for yourself and your life and your obligations as well as others and their lives and their obligations. You will circle your gardens rather than letting them corner you. You will change the channel and listen more to your creation and creativity than to your to-do list. You will know you are in a spiritual practice of putting God first and Mammon second when you are content. You will proudly refer to yourself as an imperfectionist—and not be bragging but instead praising. You will know your spiritual practice by the joy and peace in your heart. That, for most of us, will be something very new and very good. And oddly, it is already right there, already given, fully accomplished by the fact of your creation. You will always be ready for your next move.

Chapter Seven

The Turn toward the Practical

In the first chapter I argued that there is a spiral nature to the practical and the spiritual, the practical and the theological. They work as a spiral with and toward each other. We do based on what we are; we are what we end up doing. More importantly, we wish that our doing and our being would be married and that we would be a whole. Often we are in parts. We value one thing and intend one thing and we do another. We sometimes feel like fakes or forgeries. In the time famine, we often give our time to that which we don't really value but instead are obligated to do. We save the fun stuff for the end of the day or time period—and often end up without the fun, so obligated are we to the duties. We say we don't have enough time or that we need an extra hour each day, just to pause or think or enjoy.

In that first chapter I also argued that there are two reasons for our disconnect between talking the talk and walking the walk. One is a quiet, if persistent, fear of dying. We don't start the day understanding that this is just one of the 26,000 or so we will be lucky to get. We start the day imagining that there will be one day after another, but there won't. The other reason is that we are double-timers. We worship both God and Mammon and are optimistic enough or prideful enough or both that we think we can do both. We can't.

We need to put one above the other for both to flourish. We can attend to Mammon, but we cannot worship it.

The antidote to these double and twining dilemmas is clearing the spirit. It is clarity about our limitations and our hopes. That clarity allows us to walk our talk. We really do want to talk the walk and walk the talk, but instead we find ourselves distanced from our best selves. St. Paul always comes in handy here: "The good that I would do, I do not, and the evil that I would not do, I do" (paraphrasing Rom 7:19). I am not saying it is evil to be divided or macerated or cut up into little parts, but it is certainly not good.

Here follow some ways to connect ourselves to ourselves. This is a method of clearing. It comes from that great psalm about wanting a new heart. It also comes from what the Quakers know how to do well: They call their meetings *clearings*. I love that idea of a meeting, and note that it is opposite from the usual meeting, which "kicks the can down the road." We can't decide what to do, so we don't decide what to do—and then we call another meeting. I love to sing a certain song satirically. You probably know it: "For He's a Jolly Good Fellow." I sing it as "They called another meeting, they called another meeting, they called another meeee-ting. That nobody can deny."

The practical advice I will give here wants to remove the satire from my song. It wants to sing a different song: "We Called Another Clearing." The sum of the advice is to go for the next step, to face the fact that we can't do all that we want to do. Or that we need to "kill" something, or, minimally, face the gap that exists in most organizations and most people most of the time. "Watch the gap" is not just something the Metro North train tells me as a warning to watch my step. When we watch the gap, we acknowledge that we might not be able to get there from here. We probably won't resolve everything in our own version of time deprivation. But we can certainly find the next step, even if the next step is acknowledging our limitations and learning how to say no to our pride or optimism about time. We can certainly imagine doing less, even if that possibility makes us feel bad or small or stupid—or all three.

Clearing is finding the next best step for the here and now. That step may be the exercise of the negative. It may mean saying no, as much as we would like to say yes. It may mean clearing the brush from the meadow that could be our life. It may mean getting rid of things. Permit me two examples.

EXAMPLE ONE

The first example comes from my magnificent garden upstate. It consists of a large vegetable garden in the front yard, four medium-sized flowerbeds behind the house, and a very fertile cold frame. I have decided to halve the garden. Yup—to cut it to half its current size. I have tried to circle the garden, as I suggested earlier. But even a good circle wasn't allowing the garden its proper tending. By the time I got back to the weeds in cycle one, they were stronger than I was.

The halving has already involved moving a bunch of daylilies from bed three up top into the other two beds. It will soon involve mowing over that bed and taking out the stones that "bordered" its excess. In the front patch, instead of twenty-four tomatoes, there will be twelve. My husband has already begun his protest, but he doesn't know what it does to my summer spirit when, in August, I can no longer weed them all and they start to collapse into each other, making an ugly mess. Halving the garden is clearing the garden. I do have some grief—and also much more gladness. I hope for clarity in the garden that will please me more than the weeds teasing me on an otherwise beautiful morning. They like to catcall and say what I forbid my grandchildren to say to each other: "Nanna nanna boo boo." The weeds and their tendrils say, "You are no good; you just think you are. You are a no-good gardener and you are wasting tomatoes." Clearing allows me to respond to the weeds' truth with something like personal integrity. I tell the weeds they are right: I can't take care of that much fertility, so I am halving the garden.

Gardening looks so easy from the vantage point of early May. The earth is barren, begging to be filled. By the end of May the gentian has arrived. By June it is joined by the sticky sweet weed that is hard to pull. By July the native grasses show up and refuse to be pulled. By August all three are in direct competition with the tomatoes, except in gardens tended by gardeners so tidy that they can't be tamed. Weeds join flowers and vegetables and the fight is on.

I am reminded of the first garden: "And the Lord God planted a garden in Eden, in the east; and there he put the man whom he had formed. Out of the ground the Lord God made to grow every tree that is pleasant to the sight and good for food, the tree of life also in the midst of the garden, and the tree of the knowledge of good and evil" (Gen 2:8–9).

I am thinking God also made the weeds with the same flamboyance that he made the mosquitoes. In fact, the theologian in me wants to know how many mosquitoes Noah took on the ark, and how he knew their genders sufficiently to assure reproduction.

I remember that some tidy gardeners, the ones who invented insecticides, tried to rid us of bugs that bite and not only failed at their objective but also caused trouble beyond their imagination. The elimination of bugs also eliminated some birds and butterflies. As noted in chapter 1, Rachel Carson's *Silent Spring* outed their foul play, calling them the "control men."

As I dedicate myself to a weed-free garden this year, I wonder if she would accuse me of being a control woman. How important are the weeds to the growth of my choices? A wise gardener once said, "Garden as though you will live forever." I wonder if this advice applies to my approach to the weeds, which is to pull them out and only grow, speaking garden-wise otherwise, what I choose to control to grow. I certainly want the vegetables, but I also want to know the difference between good and evil.

My grandfather grew two crops, year in and year out, on a hill in what is now uptown Kingston, New York, thirty miles north of where mine is now. He grew strawberries and potatoes, and it was my job to weed them. I hated weeding. But then I was only ten, and weeding was a job. There was one good week for weeding: the week when the berries were ripe. We were to weed and pick at the same time, and could eat all we wanted. But had we not done all the weeding before the sweetening, we would have had less sweet.

It's going to be a rough year for some of the nectarines and peaches: the stone fruits, we call them. That frost that came after an early warming put them in danger. It also appears to have turned my lilac blossoms black. Neither control men nor control women could stop the frost that came unbidden. I am trying to figure out if it is really true that people plant fruit trees fully aware that they will never eat the fruit they plant. Gardening is an oddball combination of control and release—and I'm still trying to get the balance right. Clarity is the same oddball combination of letting go and taking on. Coming to terms with a measurement for what we can maintain—and learning to love, rather than hate, the art of maintaining—really matters. I mentioned meetings earlier. What I know about meetings is that every meeting I take will require another 20 percent of whatever time the thing took to administer it. I will have to follow up. I will have to alert people who weren't there what happened. I will have to decide a measurement for how much time I can give to this meeting's project. So I like to think of meetings as 120 percent of what they say they are. It helps me value their weeding, their maintenance.

All of us have been fed from fields we did not till. We also cross bridges we did not build and sit in the shade of trees we did not plant. All of us have the great gifts of our forebears. Without my grandfather teaching me how easy it is to grow potatoes and strawberries, I might have missed a lot of peanut butter and jelly sandwiches—not to mention the potato salad. We gardeners can make believe we are in charge, but we also know that we are just kidding. Another wise, if unknown, garden guru argued that gardening is better than therapy—and you also get tomatoes. We both cultivate the garden and are cultivated by it. Would it be just as easy to buy strawberries already packaged bright in boxes? Yes. Would it be just as easy to buy potatoes in plastic mesh bags, already somewhat washed? Of course. And why not wait for the other gardeners to have too many tomatoes and purchase them as well? We could do that. But then we would never get to weed our own gardens, and that would be throwing us into a control game, the kind wisely weeded people learn to avoid.

Dealing with the time famine is not a control game, and it doesn't involve killing off songbirds. It has to do with weeding and going to meetings and getting a measure in our own hearts of how much we can do. I need to halve my garden. Maybe you need to double yours. I don't know. But I do know that double-timing doesn't work and that clear timing does.

Be sure to check in with me in August to see if I got the weeds to stop their catcalling. I may or may not succeed in quieting their fuss, but I intend to try.

A SECOND, BRIEFER EXAMPLE

Learning how to say no is not a small thing. When we double-time life, everyone, including us, knows that we won't succeed in our objective. Something will drop. It might be something important that drops. It may even make a big fat mess on the floor or out of our lives. So first of all, actively saying no beats passively saying no. Passive negatories hurt people's feelings and use up time that could be spent on praise and fun.

In any given week, twice the number of people want a pastoral appointment with me than I can see. I have learned to say, with eye contact, "I am so sorry that I can't see you this week. I really am. I can see you in a month, and if you don't want to wait that long, here are some people who could probably see you sooner." The practical gift is the clearing, the realization that I just can't see more than six people a day and that I should really only see four. That is my people diet's best nourishment. You don't want to be the sixth on a day that has already seen five, had three meetings, and so on. I won't be good to you or for you. I might even start to doze while you are pouring your heart out. Why would I do that to you? I would do that because I was sinning by imagining I could do way more than I can. I mentioned earlier that I like to tell people I used to be able to do the work of three people and now can do only the work of two. I have learned the hard way—by hurting people's feelings—to make only those promises I can keep and to avoid promises I can't keep. I really mean it when I say I am sorry as prelude to the no.

I also know how to advance the calendar. My business is easy compared to most people's businesses. I can keep my own calendar. I can limit even hard cases to six appointments in a row. I only do four premarital sessions; I used to do six. I only do forty-five-minute appointments; I used to do an hour. Why? Because I know the e-mail tax on time. In the same way that meetings are 120 percent of what people think they are, counseling appointments are 25 percent more. In my world today, if I am off e-mail for more than an hour at a time, I get behind—way behind. As I will argue in the next section, I don't want my e-mails to join my weeds in wagging their fingers at me and mocking me. I strive to keep up with them so that I remove that permission from them. If I do forty-five-minute appointments, I can go on the computer and maybe even take a little break before the next one. It's like halving the garden. It is a way of saying no so that you can say yes to what is otherwise going to bug you. Yes, there is a control woman speaking here. Time management involves active control, not hurtful control. Control is a good thing when we control *how* we control. It becomes a bad thing when it turns into worry or abuse of others. When we commit to more than we can accomplish and promise more than we can deliver, we are passively agreeing to disappoint the very people we might want to please with a vigorous honesty and a full self. You can be a gardener and a pastor if you get clear about your size. It is not God's size. It is your size.

WHO IS TECHNOLOGY TO YOU?

Most people agree that technology has become way too big for its britches. It reaches into places where it doesn't belong. It gives us great power and great angst. It can give the great happiness of a really good podcast or great music on demand as well as the great anxiety of being pelleted by personal messages that basically say to us, "You're not enough the way you are; you need me and what I have to offer."

When we move out of the double-timing lies we tell ourselves, we let our e-mail become just e-mail. It is a form of cultural expression that glues us to our devices and our phones, and often makes us miserable. It is a thing. It is a robot. It is a means, not an end. We don't have to treat it nicely. We can put it in its place. I keep my e-mails to twenty in the inbox per day and delete or archive all the rest. I also give very brief responses to a lot of people. People call it the curt approach; I call it survival. Many say I have taken perfunctory to new levels, and I agree. I have decided to do just that. If I didn't, a lot of other people would be running my life instead of me. And I would be more busy than I want to be or really can be. I want to live the life I choose. I choose the life I have. It does involve a whirl, a very active whirl. But it is my choice, and that makes a big difference. I know what happens to me when I direct my energy toward pleasing others. It is not pretty. I probably am writing this book because I know *so much* about the time famine and its pain.

I had a glimpse of the consequences of my double-timing just recently. The new knobs we had purchased for our stove didn't fit, and they had to be returned. The new socks we ordered also didn't fit. They were short when they should have been long, so they also had to be returned. I sent the socks back to the stove manufacturer and the knobs back to the sock manufacturer. The lady from the sock company in Minnesota gave "Minnesota nice" a new dimension: "Mrs. Schaper, what would you like me to do with the stove knobs?"

I haven't heard from the stove company yet about the socks.

To understand the moral and actual appeal of clearing, you have to do something as seemingly mistaken as send your hopes about yourself to yourself. You have to please the right person, which is you. You can't send your knobs to the sock people and your socks to the knob people. We often look for peace and clarity in all the wrong places.

We all know technology was supposed to help us and free us from effort and hard work. Most of us are amazed at how original our sin is. We seem to *want* to be obligated and to work harder than we need to do.

Don't get me wrong: If we had full individual power over the commands of technology, we might treat it better and let it treat us better. There are powerful social, economic, and cultural forces at work. The energy behind the "not enough" messages that prevail is well organized and smart.

I'll tell you a story. I almost missed a plane last week. I thought it was a 10:48 departure, but it was a 10:38 departure, so I was walking around in the waiting area doing people watching when the attendants at the gate yelled my name. Oh, no! I rushed to the gate, which wasn't far. One of the attendants said, "You just strolled to the gate. You've been strolling around for a long time. I've seen you." I felt accused, out of compliance with my commanding officer's orders: No strolling in the airport! You are to rush on our behalf! Hmmm. Somebody also complimented me recently on the way I "run" the church. I now notice that word everywhere: "Can she run an organization?" To really run an organization in a way that honors time and self, we should *not* run an organization, nor should run to the gates as the doors threaten to close. I believe in walking an organization, sometimes even in strolling an organization. Why would we want to run it? Where do we think we are going? Unfortunately, the commandment to rush is everywhere. And e-mails lead the pack in the messaging: Open me! Open me now!

Max Zahn reports on an interesting question: "Why the current cultural fetish for zombies? In 2014's Hooked, Nir Eyal ventures a guess: 'Perhaps technology's unstoppable progress—ever more pervasive and persuasive—has grabbed us in a fearful malaise at the thought of being involuntarily controlled'" ("Zen and the Art of Zombie Killing").

Zahn notes that Eyal may have a point: We check our phones every 4.3 minutes. Kai Ryssdal on NPR's *Marketplace* says that there are eight deaths a day in the United States due to distracted driving. We all know what that means.

No one can resist these temptations by the sole use of willpower. That would be another form of lying, and I am giving practical spiritual direction here. Neither bootstraps nor willpower nor individual advice: That very direction of personal responsibility got us into this mess in the first place. We believe that effort will get us what we want and need, and it will not. More effort and more obligation to more effort is the root of the problem. We need to live in a more beautiful dimension, that of gift and enchantment, not effort and obligation. Every good deed we are able to perform is a gift. We can even gift e-mails to each other as opposed to whipping ourselves into a frenzy in order to answer them.

We rightly use the language of addiction when it comes to e-mail. Some argue for *unplugging*, language that turns the human being into a machine. Like the language "burnt out," we imagine ourselves as batteries or machines. We aren't batteries or machines. We are people. People make choices. We know we are creatures of a loving God or if not that at least a loving something that powers a great universe. Eyal continues, "The split-second attention economy establishes the battleground of consumer capitalism in the most intimate place of all: the mind." He offers Buddhism and mindfulness as alternative ways of being. Buddhism argues that human beings are bundles of unfillable needs. It is futile to imagine an endgame with e-mail or technology. We cannot satisfy human wants by feeding them, thus we tame them. We limit them. We add fullness of mind to the emptiness that comes from fulfilling needs. Mindfulness is not willpower; it is letting go of the power of the will to will. It is a delightful emptiness, almost as liberating as an empty inbox.

Interestingly, Buddhism is rapidly growing in popularity in places like the Silicon Valley. Zahn writes, "'There's a growing awareness among [techies] that their minds are insane,' said Vince Horn, founder of a podcast and online community called Buddhist Geeks that examines the intersection of Buddhism and technology. 'Insanity is directly proportional to the number of hours spent at a tech startup.' In Horn's view, techies turn to Buddhism, especially the practice of mindfulness, because it calms them down."

Calm is a very expensive feeling. Individual developments like meditation and gardening and walking or just strolling in an airport surely help. But absent a full-scale political, economic, and cultural change, individuals will still be in time trouble in this nation. Many simply have to join the technological rat race. Opting out is a viable option only for the privileged. This is not something political I am saying; it is true. Most of us know it much too well. There may be some art in personal forgery—looking your best, adopting a great style, doing your best. But in this country, at this time, we are addicted, and we are addicted because we are dominated. Isn't it great that in zombie movies the zombies always find a way to prevail?

SPIRITUAL FORGERY

In *When a Lie Is Not a Sin: The Hebrew Bible's Framework for Deciding*, a book I recommend highly, Rabbi Dennis Ross says that lying is not a sin when we break into the truth of why we lied in the first place. Often the intention of the lie is to be better than we are and to dress up into our best selves rather than going out into the world in our sweats and T-shirts. The lie is personal design, it is intention, and it is untangling into the truth or leaning into the light. It is a lie that we can have, do, or be it all. When we say that we aren't going to participate in that lie any longer—or when we at least try not to and to aim elsewhere—we are leaning into the light and untangling the tangled truth. We are aiming to be singular about our time and ourselves and to stop the double-timing. We know that we are involved in a spiritual forgery, and we tell each other the truth about why. We are caught. We are being manipulated. And it hurts.

In Noah Charney's book *The Art of Forgery: The Minds, Motives, and Methods of the Master Forgers*, he asks a lot of good questions about art forgery. He began with the *Young Hare* by Albrecht Dürer, which was presented falsely to the museum director whom Charney describes in the book as an original when it was just a good reproduction. The museum director explained that Dürer's watercolors, *Young Hare* and *Tuft of Grass*, are shown to the public only a couple of times a year; at all other times they are stored in temperature-, light-, and humidity-controlled Solander boxes. Maybe art is as delicate as we humans are; we too need controlled circumstances to survive.

Charney went into a kind of agony because he wasn't going to be able to see the Durer originals, asking readers, "What if you booked a ticket to a show weeks in advance, only to arrive on a day when the originals were hibernating?" I want to ask this question spiritually. What part of your original is hibernating on any given day? Are you and I just very fine reproductions of our restored or original selves? And so what if we are? Does that mean God is sad about us, or just hoping we come out of our boxes and into our beauty? And what if we can only do that a couple of times a year? Would that mean we weren't really beautiful?

Charney argues, knowing how much museums keep hidden, that the only right thing to do is not to mislead. Quality reproductions, clearly labeled so that no one is fooled, play an important role in the globalization and democratization of the study of art. Not everyone can afford to fly to see original work in other countries beyond; such art can be admired and analyzed only in print or digital reproductions.

Charney writes, "A team of scientists took around 6,000 photographs, effectively scanning the entire original cave [of the Caverne du Pont D'Arc in the Ardeche region of France], in order to produce a replica that can be visited by the public, and which offers a nearly identical experience to visiting the original. This new cave simulacrum is a three-dimensional parallel to the Albertina's Dürers. . . . [The art in the cave dates] from some 36,000 years ago. In order to preserve the Chauvet cave paintings from deterioration, they are closed to all but a select few researchers" ("A Fake of Art"). Now the world can see their beauty—no longer original, but instead connected and opened and distributed, they are more than original. Our spiritual destination is to be more than unique. It is to be uniquely authentic, the full genomic self that God intended, which is you and only you, and then to be real and part of the whole, not just stranded in some box or cave. It is to come out and into our full humanity: as parts, not whole; as clear, not clean; as solo but not separated.

There is a fugitive character to these opportunities to be real and to be seen and to live by the grace of creation. You can be very glamorous on a dating site, too. You can construct an online platform that just about every-body would want to date.

If art critics and King David's psalm both think it is important to get to a clean and clear heart, I wonder how we do that in a world of great capacity to make high-quality reproductions? I even wonder if there is a new psalm waiting to be written: "Create in me a high-quality reproduction of the self I want to be?" We hybrids are on our way to being both more and less than we can be. We hybrids are on our way to doing both more and less than we can do. We hybrids are on our way to having both more and less than we can have. We are on our way, and we probably won't arrive—because, glorious-ly, we don't have enough time. But what time we do have is wonderfully truthful about and to itself.

Some of us don't forge so much as get forged. People so strongly think we are what we aren't that we have very little hope of jumping their fence. I think of Black Lives Mattering or a woman who gets cursed in her workplace for being "too angry" or some "selfish" immigrant who works all day long to build the economy only to be told on TV at night that he is ruining it. Getting clear about the lies being told to us about us is as important as not lying to ourselves.

This whole matter of privacy and presentation of self and our capacity to lie attends the question of terrorism, so dependent as it is on surprise and secrecy. ISIS finally is a crisis of meaning for people. They don't know how to move into hybrid religion or how to be multiple or how to be more than one thing at a time. They are still people wanting to read this text as getting clean as opposed to getting clear. And also, there is no *they*. There is a *we* who want to tell our truth to ISIS and say we are only sort of bad as they think we are. We too have been dating Bathsheba, and no one knew until everyone knew. The only real solution to terrorism will be truth telling in a safe enough environment that everything and everybody has a good confes-sion and a good cry. We have to tell the truth to each other about who we are and who we aren't, about when our forged and fake mode is on display and when it is not.

The matter of privacy in truth telling is important. The most important person to tell the truth to is you. You may not need, as Ross argues, to tell all your truth to everybody all the time. You could argue that such truthfulness might become a kind of forgery itself, or that nobody has time for that much of you. In the multiple computer-driven issues around protecting identity and privacy so that there is a thing called *privacy* left somewhere, there is also so much that isn't being said. There is an Orwellian kind of lie hidden in all this openness: My cell phone seems to know how to find me no matter where I am. No wonder so many teenagers have two phone accounts. Maybe another split in us is the desire to be alone and to be together, to be in community without having to attend a lot of meetings, to take a long hike and not feel too alone. A person who knows the grace of God knows how to be alone and together. He or she also knows that we have been forged or that our time has been invaded, counted, measured by forces that may or may not have our best interests at heart. Capitalism is a strong economic system, with strong economic interests, which may or may not be in our best interest or in the interest of those we love or those about whom we feel guilty or helpless.

Here is an expensive question: Why, if capitalism is so difficult, are you and I so weak that we can't even tame it? The answer will cost you spiritual currency but save you material currency.

A lie is not a sin when it is you who have been forged. A lie is not a sin when you tell people you are lying: "I work here for the money." A lie is not a sin when we engage the truth at multiple levels and tell people we are putting our best foot forward when we say whatever we just said. We are trying to be truthful as we try to become clear.

CLEAR, NOT CLEAN

In the first chapter I argued that the word *clean* needs to become the word *clear*. Even Jamaica Kincaid—one of my absolute favorite authors—needs to get the point. She objects to daffodils, because they are not native to her place, and tells a whole anticolonial story through something yellow in a novel called *Lucy*. Why can't daffodils travel, like people or art travel, to get more clear, to get less phony, to get rid of the ideas of purity and cleanliness that so mightily threaten us? Is there really that much truth to the one original or the one painting or even the one marvelous folk culture? Are we not all quality reproductions of our parents and schools and lovers and friends? These mixtures and hybrids are only wrong when we mislead and say they aren't there. They are beautiful when they are untangled and untwisted and unsnarled. When cleared, they become the restoration of the joy of our salvation. The truth about where we are now and who we are now becomes a spiritual GPS. We don't have to hate technology. We have to use it and keep it from using us. We have to tame it. We may have to learn to say no, if and as we can. We may be able to halve our garden and enjoy it twice as much. We may become more artful forgeries.

I will never be free of my participation in capitalism, nor of its participation in me. I will never know fully how to stop wanting, being, or having it all. I may learn how to be truthful about me and mine. I will learn when I accept the gift of having enough time.

I will attend Mammon and worship God.

Chapter Eight

The Importance of Numbers

In chapter 2, I talked about Noah's response to God's great judgment. He numbered the animals and brought them two by two on an ark. Perhaps he couldn't fit any more? Was he wise enough to know his limits, count his capacity, and befriend his human capacity? My theory unites both the size of his ark and the wisdom he showed. Wisdom acknowledges capacity. In the great words of guru Stephen Covey, we identify our circle of influence—what we can realistically manage—and distinguish it from our circle of concern—what we care about but know we can't manage. We may really care about a lot of things but have the capacity to actually attend to only a few.

I love the advice in Psalm 90—"So teach us to number our days, that we may apply our hearts unto wisdom; O satisfy us early"—that we number our days. The most practical thing I know to do is to enumerate my capacities. I have a Donna cycle, which goes like this. Each day I do ten things. Some days I even evaluate whether I do those ten things. Three attend to my health: walk in the morning, do a customized yoga in the morning, and in the afternoon do something aerobic. Yes, I cheat on these matters and do quickies when the full objective of a long walk, a full practice of postures, and two hours of tennis don't all fit. I still use them as touchstones, ways to count whether I am living as a body in a body. I do three work things, four appointments, an hour of e-mail (keeping the inbox to twenty items or less), and then I meditate and strategize. I don't do Buddhist meditation; I do active meditation. I think. I believe reflection is more than important to action. Action without reflection is stupid; action with reflection is choice filled. I do two domestic things: paying attention to grooming and to my houses, which I clean in a corner method, spiraling through the whole place about once a month. (I also employ a gal Friday who gets free room in our house and cleans weekly.)

I also like to write for an hour a day. I am an avocational writer with a half dozen regular assignments. I also cycle and circle and spiral these. Finally, because I am of a certain age and a technological dinosaur, once a day I try to learn something new on my phone or computer or in the use of social media. For me it's like learning Spanish or Greek.

In an evaluative mode, I might give a thousand points to each of these activities, with the possibility of a a ten-thousand-point day, which is Donna optimum and ideal. I hover around six thousand, year in and year out. I've been hoping for this ten-thousand-point day to regularize for about a decade now. It is rarely achieved, but always a destination. I do have the capacity for the ten-thousand-pointer and am often interrupted on my way to my ideal capacity.

In the summer I enjoy many more ten-thousand-point days than in the working seasons. I live upstate then and go to work only three days a week, with the freedom and the self-management potential of doing most work electronically.

The TENS

Morning Walk. In New York: all three parks (Gramercy, Union Square, and Washington Square). Upstate: climb the mountain behind our house. All with my peppy border collie, Sybil.

Yoga Postures. I have a custom-designed set of six postures, which is not much but is lots of fun.

E-mail. This one often expands, edging out the walk and the yoga and the grooming and the domestic delights.

Domestic Clearing/Cleaning/Touching/Enjoying. If all I can do on any given day is water one plant, that is what I do.

Grooming. Loving the shower and the clothes choices and the earrings.

Writing for an Hour.

Ideally, these six are done by noon if I get up at six.

Work from 12–9. Real work with real people.

Aerobic Exercise. Scheduled somewhere during the work time.

Meditation and Strategizing. Again, scheduled during the nine hours of office time. I am lucky to have a park outside my office door, which I visit frequently.

Techno Time.

As anyone who is a professional knows, work expands to fill the time you give it. You see what a breakfast meeting can do or what havoc evening meetings can develop. I almost never have these ten-thousand-point days in a row. (The reason for the thousands as numbers is so you can say how much you missed or achieved in a given segment.) I also work six or seven days most weeks and take off a long day, long enough to find the time for ten thousand points of activity, every couple of weeks. I also take a five-minute nap on most days—and on a long day, I get a longer nap. I choose this schedule. I number my days as if each day has a little vacation time built into it. I am living the life I want, and that gives me the energy for a "big" schedule. I like to work 120 percent of the time instead of just 100 percent of the time. I like the stretch and the challenge of it. Others may not. Again, numbers are important; you should live by yours.

This is a Donna schedule; it is not yours. The point is not to imitate my schedule so much as to develop your own. So: teach us to number our days, that our hearts are applied to wisdom. I believe in counting and personal evaluation. You may want a less clumsy approach. What wisdom advocates is to have a pattern to which you can be personally accountable, which is doable, and which shows up in your heart regularly.

WISDOM

A friend said to me that he had a confession to make: "I loaned my friend a thousand dollars and he hasn't paid me back. I have now lost both a friend and a thousand dollars." His distress was so acute that I wanted to rush immediately to advice: "Don't you know the folk wisdom about lending money to friends or families? Never do it. Either give it straight out if you really want to help or say no. But don't lend it. The person who borrowed it is likely to not be able to pay it back, and then you will have this kind of double loss." But I resisted advice and rested in wisdom. In wisdom you can rest and be released of some of the anxiety of doubling or tripling losses or even just plain empathy for your friend. You don't have to solve his problem. You just have to hear it, acknowledge it, and listen to it. You don't have to carry it.

Folk wisdom is often better than language classes or book learning or yoga. Education is great and classes are wonderful—but they often tell us less than we need to know. The psalm tries to teach us to "so number our days, that we may apply ourselves unto wisdom." We are to apply ourselves to wisdom. And the folk wisdom about giving not lending to friends or families is widely appreciated. As wisdom, it stands the test of time. We may really want to help our friend. We may have enough money to share. If we give it and not lend it, we become wiser. Wisdom is different than smarts. Wisdom more often avoids tragedy. Wisdom gives the self permission to have its own way, not the other ways that others want it to have. When you are wise, you custom design your own days, your own ways. Like Noah, you choose who you bring on your ark.

Some people steal time from us, causing us to worry about them instead of about ourselves. As a general rule, very few people are in your circle of influence about whom you do not care fundamentally. Your partner, your children, your boss, and your employees: they are people about whom you must and may care.

People who clog your emotional inbox may be in your circle of concern, but they don't need to get in any further.

Most of us know the folk wisdom "Neither a borrower nor a lender be." My friend could have used that advice earlier in his career as a lender. He went outside his circle of concern, his arc of caring, instead of staying within his circle of influence.

Wisdom applies to the environment as well. Many of us find large subjects moving into our lives and our emotional inboxes. We care about many things about which we are clearly powerless: terrorism, global warming, poverty, or Syrian refugees. Noah faced this same dilemma when he saw the grave threat to the world as he knew it. He counted and calculated his response. One of my favorite people is eighty-five years old, and she calls or writes a different legislator every morning. She cares for these people who represent her, and they and their secretaries know her care. She is a very effective lobbyist, "bird by bird," in the famous words of Anne Lamott. When asked how she wrote so many great books and blog posts, she responded, "Bird by bird," meaning word by word. My friend is not saving all the Syrian refugees, but she will save one or two. She has chosen her vocation and does what she can with what she has. Most of us don't do what we can with what we have because we are so worried about all that we can't do. We refuse to count our capacity. We forget the animals on the ark, going two by two, or the writing, bird by bird. When we number our days, we approach wisdom.

A friend has given the environment to us. We don't have to pay it back. You and I may differ about which kind of creator made the rivers and paths, the creeks and the meadows. But neither of us thinks it was us. We were given what we call *nature*. We did not create it. But it has not been loaned to us and we need not worry about paying it back. It is instead a gift. There is a difference, and this difference has to do with becoming our right size, not our grandiose size.

Jane Jacobs, the extraordinary activist in Greenwich Village, who held development at bay in New York City and fussed effectively with Robert Moses, would have been one hundred years old in 2016. She extended landmark protections to the village and let it continue to look more like a town than a city. She argued for human-scaled neighborhoods that emphasized street life. She defended the small against the big. Ironically, when we loan money to friends or try to pay our own way, we go big when instead we should stay small. The spiritual roots of the environmental crisis are here: We lost wisdom and went big when we should have stayed small.

Knowing that we are creatures as well as creatives will help the environment shift to sustainability much more than our little idolatries of thinking we can do more than we can. Staying small and refusing the big will also help.

Before our breath is genuinely taken away, we can number our days and apply them to wisdom. At least we can stop being lenders, if we can't also stop being borrowers. We can listen to folk wisdom as if we *were* folk, and not above folk. Sweep your own side of the street. It is not your business. There are a lot of great pieces of wisdom that we all know and have all said before. Maybe it's time to listen to each other. The folk way of saying this is that we have one mouth and two ears. Listening can be much more important than speaking. Receiving can be as important as giving.

We can refuse to overdo on behalf of doing. We can refuse to over-be on behalf of being. Perhaps we plant half the garden, or declutter our inbox, or forgo the people about whom we can do nothing, the causes about which we can do little. The small numbering of e-mails becomes the route to the large and lovely. They become our personal ark, and eventually a rainbow and a dove.

DOES NOAH BUG YOU?

Maybe we are all Noahs—or at least our nightmares are his. Like Noah, we have become aware of God's wrath. We have a sense of insufficient time to please God, so busy are we pleasing others. Like Noah, we have heard the instruction to do something. We have wondered what took God so long to get mad. We have left a lot behind. We are on the ark, wondering what will happen next. The rain comes down; it lasts more days than we can count. Then the world is drenched, or at least our spiritual imagination is. We long for a bow in the sky, a dove on the tree.

Part of us goes back to work. We become more serious activists and more serious slacktivists. We click and clack on one "like" after another. We pray, then we pray some more. There is no bow yet in the sky and no dove to be seen.

Nights can be long, even countless, which is both a natural and a secular kind of nightmare. They can be long enough to think about Noah. Was it a miracle or was it a miracle plus that saved Noah and the animals from the flood? Was it God being extravagant? Did God restore the earth, or did we? Or was it a partnership? I think the latter. If I didn't, I'd never get any sleep.

Nobody wants to worship a punishmentalist God: one that chooses one man and his family and not another's, who saves one while letting the rest drown. Nor does anybody want to worship a putzy permissive God, one who lets humanity scorch the earth and doesn't care enough to act. Instead we want a God who loves us without setting conditions. We want a God who cares enough to stop us from hurting each other, while simultaneously not giving up on our power to change our own ways. We want a God who is a giver, who is large enough to get over being furious with us for not appreciating the gift.

Repentance can be cheap. "So sorry," we say to Mother Earth or her children who live in low lands. Then we get back in our cars. Repentance— the kind we buy with night thoughts—can also be expensive. Repentance can require something of us. That kind of metanoia, or turning, that life-changing participation is important. It is what Noah did, without fully knowing what he was doing. How *could* he know what he was doing? Wisdom doesn't know; it simply orients. In the psalm about numbering our days, we are to head toward satisfaction. We can't know if we are there until we make a reasonable, realistic assessment of our direction.

There is nothing easy about following in Noah's footsteps. Why Noah? Why not somebody else? There is such a slippery slope here theologically. Many activists and people who want to do good align themselves with Noah thinking that they are Noah, only to find out that God has chosen another Noah. What if we aren't Noah? We have to be so careful here not to think we can earn our own sleep or our own salvation or our own peace of planet or peace of mind. God acts; we follow. We don't know if we are among the drowning or the floating. We can't purchase our safety in the great sea of life. The Noah story may help us with climate change or bring us back to time feast—as long as we don't turn the story into our story alone. We don't earn God's favor by being better people. We earn God's favor by doing what God tells us to do, even if the divine instructions are more than a little micromanaging. Really, what does God know about cubits? How big is our ark? How much could we do if we let ourselves relax into the grace of partnership with God? What if we got out of our own way? What if we could be doing more, not less? Wisdom let us ask these questions in a relaxed way. The questions don't have answers so much as a great opportunity for trial and error. Why not experiment with a graceful enumeration of yourself? There is salvation for all, even the unchosen. There is frequently sentimentality around Noah and the ark and its story: warm fuzzy animals, the elephants, the toy boats. The second you see the story as a life-and-death matter, for you and not others or for others and not you, you *de*-sentimentalize. You wonder whether the story really is a good one for children or not.

WHO KNOWS HOW LONG WE HAVE OR DON'T HAVE?

When you wake in the long night, consider: Is climate damage a divine punishment for corruption, or is it the result of our agency? In other words, did we do this to ourselves? God seems to think yes, and still he sets a bow in the sky. Is that bow a miracle or something like a miracle plus, an extra that God gives because God can—like the thirteenth bagel in the dozen we paid for? I think the latter, and I am building an ark. The are no guarantees that I will be saved or that you will be saved, but when I go to my final sleep I'd like to think I was on the side God intended from the beginning, in that place where day and night never cease. "As long as the earth endures, seedtime and harvest, cold and heat, summer and winter, day and night will never cease" (Gen 8:22) is the end of the story of Noah and the ark. Maybe that promise is the beginning. For me it has been the beginning of living in forty-day cycles of trouble and pleasure, of thinking in seasonal ways, of learning to live between the moons rather than above or outside them. The promise has to do with taking God's micromanagement about cubits feet and the size of the ark. What size is the ark we have? Can we measure it? Can we number it? Why? Why not?

HOW MUCH STUFF DO YOU NEED?

It is not an accident that the word *sustainable* is so popular that it's almost out of fashion. We know that we are living unsustainable lives, and we long to live sustainably. We know there are sacred cycles to time, and that there are organizational cycles as well. We even know that we seem to age while we aren't looking and are almost always changing. We know that change, not permanence, is normal. We might even love evolution and pray for its sustainability rather than its interruption.

Our hyperproductive mode, in which time is only a raw material of production, has taken us to the brink of destruction. In a world that discards meditation or peace as—literally—a waste of time, nuclear war, destruction of the ozone layer, acid rain, deforestation, and global warming are all inevitable. These awful "floods" of spirit and nature are caused by our hyperproductive modes. The flood and the rainbow remind us that we may and must renew the cycles and our celebration of them in order to live.

One of the ways we participate in this lack of sustainability is in our homemaking. I first became the kind of radical I am about the time I realized that people were constantly saying to me, "My house is a mess." I realized they weren't kidding, and I wanted to know why people with big mortgages had messy houses. I wanted to know why the American dream of a detached house with a two-car garage had become polluted by clutter. I love being a homemaker, a domestic. I have a device that cuts oranges so you can put votive candles in them for holidays. I overdo domesticity, and often wish I didn't. I have been called the Martha Stewart of spirituality or the Henry Ford of politics. I have my quirks. And I have little clutter.

What is clutter? Clutter is stuff you don't need. It is stuff that has lost its function. In a home, it could be books that need dusting or reading, a chair that the cat scratched up right before she died, a drawer full of graters in multiple sizes, a second egg beater (just in case the first one breaks). My votive maker is not clutter. I love it. I use it. But I also don't think everyone needs one. They can borrow mine if they're having a party.

In a church, clutter may be the well-loved stuffed animals in the nursery school or the costumes from the very popular Christmas pageant of 2006. It may also be financial records dating back to 1947 or the full set of minutes from the now-defunct Ladies' Aid Society. Clutter is often found in those anachronistic filing cabinets, all of which can and should be digitalized on behalf of a well-remembered past and a brighter future.

You really don't need those filing cabinets, nor do you really need to alarm parents of toe-dippers in the Sunday school about germs or dust. You may need those books at home for company, but they don't need to make you sneeze when you pick them up. What we need is high-functioning space. I work in a church, so I will use it as an example.

Those who administer sacred places are even more alert to the importance of their functions than those in other organizations. We exist to love and praise God and to love and praise God forever. When it looks like we have forgotten how to love God's house, we may be witnessing the opposite of our missional function. It may be good to have a cluttered attic or basement or closet in a home you call your own, but in a sacred site, too much attention to the past can give a message you don't choose: It may say you are more interested in what *was* than in what *can be*.

In her very large house, another friend of mine kept one large room that she called her "unconscious." There she tossed all the things she couldn't throw away, leaving them there for her sons and me to throw away. The room was knee deep in earrings, books, jeans, shirts, and unopened mail. We had a ball as soon as we rented the dumpster.

Marie Kondo's *The Life-Changing Magic of Tiding Up: The Japanese Art of Decluttering and Organizing* is a best-seller for a reason. A lot of us have stuff following us around that we no longer need. It represents stale energy, the kind that mold loves to attach itself to. Mold makes things moldy. At home, we may wonder about that old bicycle that needs new tires. We may decide to either ride it or donate it. At church, we may want the kitchen to smell of the last baked bean supper, because that smell reminds us how much fun the next one will be. We may not want to spend the next council meeting wondering why the air feels so well used. We may be glad some volunteers did a fall cleanup, but we don't want to see the lawn mower or Weedwacker left on the lawn.

Congregations are uniquely positioned to love their sacred space. We want the very best for them, and that's why we used to have altar guilds to attend to the freshest flowers and most well-ironed linens. We may want the banners to be gorgeous during Advent, the four candles brand new. We may, if we are lucky enough to be chosen to clean up after communion, wash the chalice and paten with much more attention than we would ever give a frying pan.

We may also be a little frugal—a word sometimes interchangeable with its sibling, *cheap*—and may purchase the cheaper plastic coffee cup because "it's for the church." Yes, we are confused about money, expense, and luxury. We aren't sure about the word *extravagant* And we also love the lovely. What might be much more beautiful and frugal and aesthetically appropriate to the sacred is to reuse that old set of China, over and over again. This is a radical act that probably won't happen because too many of the same people have been stuck too long washing the dishes. Then again, if we were Benedictine, we could be more radical. We would honor housekeeping and homemaking as much as we honor the choir and the preacher. Benedictines make an annual schedule and award people with the opportunity to wash the coffee hour dishes once a year: "Oh, wow, it's my turn!" We could give prizes to the people who have the most fun doing so. Paper products are not green and take up most of the closet space. They make the art of hospitality look convenient and portable. By these choices we don't only clutter up our space and hurt the environment we love; we also bow at the altar of convenience while preaching the art of care. Why high-priced convenience? Because we fear we don't have enough time. And truth is, we *don't* have enough time, so busy are we being convenient. We have plenty of time. What we don't have is beautiful time in beautiful spaces, where we can relax and be satisfied.

At home we have daily opportunities to clean and corner. I both love and hate housecleaning. As long as I call it housekeeping or homemaking, I am able to do it. As I said in the first part of this chapter, I live on a housekeeping spiral rather than schedule. I clean a corner a day, starting with any cobwebs that might be up top, dusting the woodwork afterward, and moving out any umbrellas I may have left there for a rainy day. It amazes me how many things I keep for a rainy day. Neither my house nor I really need this rain gear. Instead I need the clarity of the corner and a way to lose the fear that somebody or something might be hiding right there in plain sight, ready to trip me. And it only costs me ten minutes a day—unless I get distracted by what I find in the corner or its drawer.

A home is as sacred a site as any church. Both deserve the blessing of the dust rag, the whisk of the broom, the daring of the dumpster. Both need to be cornered, lest they corner us.

RETHINKING SUNDAY MORNING OR
HOW WE KEEP A GOOD SABBATH

Religious sociologists tell us that a lot of people fib about how often they attend church. The average American worships sixteen times per year: Jews somewhat less, Christians somewhat more. If someone has counted other faiths, I don't know their results. All through this chapter I have been arguing that counting matters. It gets us to human size and creates realistic expectations for us.

Many people have passively rethought their Sabbath-keeping. They stay in bed and snuggle the children or they attend a sports event or they go out to brunch. We live in a postworshipping world. People who want to practically achieve a Sabbath-keeping practice need to figure out what we want. If congregational life does not satisfy, change your congregation or your pattern, or both. Understanding what Sabbath is will help. Sabbath is time for God, not Mammon.

Here follow ten simple ways to keep a good Sabbath.

1. Attend a different congregation every week until you find one you love. Sabbath involves community! You need people to help you keep Sabbath.

2. On your Sabbath day listen to a great church or a great synagogue worship. I go to Riverside in New York, digitally, often. I go to Rome-mu as well. I go to Trinity Church in Chicago regularly. Why not? I work on Sundays. I need another kind of Sabbath.

3. Choose some music that reminds you of God. Hum to it for a half hour whenever you feel like it.

4. Buy some great prayer books or look them up online. *The Book of Common Prayer* is superb. My little book *Prayers for People Who Say They Can't Pray* is also interesting.

5. Take a Sunday Sabbath hike or walk. Go the same place every week or to a different place every week. Go to some water you love or take in a view that inspires you.

6. Eat a great meal with people you love. Call it Sunday dinner, even if is Tuesday breakfast.

7. Pray in the morning and in the evening, every day. Let these mini-observances become your Sabbath.

8. Get a mezuzah and put it on your door. A mezuzah is a Jewish symbol that "guards your coming in and your going out, from this day forward" (Ps 121:8). Touch it when you leave and when you come home.

9. Take a long nap on Sunday afternoon.

10. Develop your own way and stick to it. Honor your custom-designed Sabbath.

NUMBERING YOUR DAYS

If we keep a good Sabbath in some measurable way and keep our homes in some measurable ways, we will find ourselves in time wisdom instead of time captivity. There is a difference. There is wisdom in numbering your days. There is wisdom in playing with points, even when you hit a 100 day in all nine categories except e-mail or technological failure. If you have long lived in the deep darkness of "never enough time," using measurements, metrics, and self-evaluation regularly and ritually can help you say, "Today, I had enough time."

Chapter Nine

Speckness

One of the reasons we stay so busy is that we want to wear the badge of busyness. We want to tattoo ourselves with importance. We want to announce to the world that we are not inconsequential; we are important. We matter. We don't not matter. We are not small but large. Like J. Paul Getty, we want the world to notice us. But most of us also know another world, a world in which we are not noticed.

In that world we push large boulders up large hills, and they tend to roll back down. Even those of us who have lots of power, like the president or the pope, contend with what they can't do on a regular basis. Parents who love their children more than earth itself know that they can't control them. Whether in the worlds of love or power—or even just trying to get across town—gridlock is a common experience. We may wear the badge of busyness but we also know how inconsequential we sometimes are.

So why do people keep trudging along in the ruts of effort and impact? Because every now and then we realize our goal. Often something does happen, but it is usually not what we had intended. Facing into our speckness—the fact of our smallness, the biological fact of less than one hundred years in a universe millions of years old—is just too disturbing. There are millions of genomic combinations, and ours is just one of them. We are so small in the large scheme of things.

There is a way to face our speckness that is empowering. Because our smallness is a fact, a biological fact, it can also be understood as a beautiful fact. This chapter is about the empowering acknowledgment of how small and useless we are. I often say, when one of my parishioners is in a lot of trouble, "May I come around and hang out and be useless with you?" This person may have lost his or her job or partner or both. His or her children may have bailed. He or she may be severely depressed. There is nothing I can do besides accompany at that point. Accompaniment is simultaneously use-less and beautiful.

Beyond the power of habit, the way we wear the badge of busyness to unsuccessfully assure ourselves of our importance, there is another hope. It is the hope for beauty, if not impact. The big word for it is *aesthetic*. By aesthetic we mean the place beyond function, cause and effect, action and consequence. We mean the things we do for the sake of doing them. We mean the "thing itself." We mean what that aesthetic movement meant when it said, "Art for art's sake." We mean refusing to answer the question of what the picture means; it means that we liked making it. We mean trying to do good without guaranteeing that good will come.

We head for the good. We aim for the beautiful. We orient toward the excellent. But we don't squeeze on the good or the beautiful or the excellent so tightly that we control them. We also get ourselves out of the way. We build the beautiful bridge not just so people can cross over the water. We build the beautiful bridge for the beautiful bridge.

In chapter 3, I argued that we often see simple common things like water in ways that are fundamentally false. We go Orwellian, or we gaslight each other. We make things be mirrors of ourselves instead of letting things be what they are. Take water, for example. Many of us think water is on earth to keep us from being thirsty, but it is not. It is here because God saw that it was good. Reread the first chapter of Genesis if you don't believe me. Of course water has functions. Of course water can be useful if portable. And above and below that, water is good. It is beautiful. It comes out of the imagination of the divine. It may even come out of the sense of humor of the divine.

For me, God is surely creator, but even more, God is artist. God is play-ful, exuberant, and in love with beauty. That's why God made us: so that we could be playful, exuberant, and in love with beauty. John Calvin put the matter in his now famous slogan, the one for which he is most known, about the most important thing to do: loving and praising God and enjoying God forever. That is God's aesthetic direction with us: why not ours with God?

We are good at tricking or condensing the truth into our historical, cultu-ral, geographic, and age frames. We even know we do it. What would my grandfather think if he saw all these people with their noses in their cell phones, as we are, just about everywhere? What if my particular genome had been born in the eighteenth century instead of the twentieth? I wouldn't be able to vote, much less be a pastor. Or what was life like before growth became yet another commandment and excess still another? How did people live before capitalism? In some ways, probably not as well as we do now, but in other ways they probably had a sense of their place in time and thought it was enough.

If we are lucky, we get three score and ten years on earth, with some of us getting more. There are millions of us here on earth now, and we will all be gone in a hundred years. New ones will come. Old ones are already gone. We are very small in the great and marvelous scheme of things. The badge of busyness won't help us be larger than we are. And we are marvelously small. God made us that way because God enjoys the smallness of us. Wearing the badge of busyness in order to be important is in direct violation of our creation. It is against the *ontos*, the way things are meant to be. So why bother? Especially since we can have so much more fun being inconsequential. Embracing the speck—the speck of you and of me—is the direction out of the time famine.

Here I argue that we are drops in the great bucket. We are sands on the great shore. We are part of a whole so large that we dare not diminish it by our own possession of it. We certainly don't want to turn God's creation into a fix-it shop, where we repair what is broken. Oddly and interestingly, when we repair what is broken, as scripture commands, we find the best route to that repair is also aesthetic. Scripture commands repair while offering a deeper peace, the ability to live with what can't be fixed, how hard we try. We act without forcing; we bend with the waters and let the waters flow through us, as us, within us, as in Tai Chi. We move through air as though it were water. We relax in time and space. We know a place. We aim for the good without becoming self-righteous about it. We keep our sense of humor. We invite people, instead of repelling them, by our joyous affirmation of the purpose of creation.

One of my favorite writers is a man named Edward Hoagland. Born in New York City, he became a circus man, working with the big cats. He had a difficult stammer and enjoyed solitude. In many of his works, he talks about the creator creating the world for the "froth." Why creation at all? Hoagland answers: For the froth of the waves in the sea. God made them, saw them, and thought they were good. And they are. If you want to consult Hoagland, try the works listed at the end of the book. They are each magnificent and point to the frothiness of the divine's intention. There is a playfulness throughout his corpus, one that allows for life principles beyond the utilitarian. We are not going to always be able to fix everything, even ourselves. We are going to join Calvin and Hoagland in living for the froth.

In what follows, I want to offer three versions of the aesthetic. These are very small ways. They are just what they are, not more and not less. They are ways of becoming more gladly a speck, using the artist's path and approach. They will be unapologetically autobiographical—as there is little point, as one speck to another, in being anything else.

A SENSE OF PLACE

We now live in both New York City and farm in Hopewell Junction, sixty miles north of the city. Our country place is just three miles north of where WNYC goes out of range, and WAMC is not in yet. A Christian fundamentalist station takes their place for three miles, giving me just a few seconds of consternation between the two homes that I love. I love this space in between, even though I am a public radio addict. Why? Because it gives me space to both depart and to arrive. Being a Christian myself, it is always amusing that another kind of Christian invades my radio so regularly.

I have long said I can only live in the country and work in the city. The homogeneity of country folk bores me stiff, and the pretense of city folk does the same. Likewise, the sturdiness of country folk and the sophistication of city folk equally amaze me. I know I am all but unsatisfiable. Don't tell the psalmist. And yet in my speck of life, I live these sixty miles as though they belong to me, acknowledging each tree and reservoir as if it were my own. It is such a patch of land, this Hudson River Valley. I love most of all taking the train down the river and getting a seat on the west side of the train. The cattails alone can keep me going for a while. They froth what is otherwise just a commute.

I never thought I would come back to the Hudson Valley. I was born here, but I always knew I would leave. Like for so many small-town kids, the point was to get out, get out soon, and never come back. Kingston was too small, too much of a speck. That thought came before I realized how provincial and small Manhattan can be.

Amherst, Massachusetts, became our home. We raised our three kids there and always thought of it as our ideal home. It was right for lots of reasons, but mostly because a church there called me to be its pastor. I was always a first, as a woman, and this was a very friendly place to be first.

I left that house and its brook-lined four acres, ten perennial gardens, fantastic soil, and deep swamp three times. The land and the house—and its mortgage, which has been underwater (an interesting Orwellian notion), for a long time—remain in Amherst, where we also raised our children and just paid $5,000 to fix the driveway. First we left for Chicago; then we came back. Then we left for Miami; then we came back. And then we left for New York City.

I became a "rurbanist." In the city I have nature deprivation syndrome; in the country I have diversity difficulties. Amherst was both very precious to me and too precious for me. I still own the house, renting it annually to UMass students who destroy it. The poppies still come up in May; the lilacs bloom right before the poppies, which are followed by the peonies. The tenants tried to pull out the asparagus but they failed—or rather, the asparagus succeeded.

The house has nineteen rooms, including four bathrooms, and a south-facing bay window. From that window, on the right snowy night, you can see a snowy owl hiding in the big fir tree, surprising you with a sense of white on evergreen that you'll not forget. My son, at age twelve, mowed a labyrinth in the back meadow. Because the meadow is lopsided, not square, the labyrinth's development required higher math and the use of one of those compasses we used to buy as schoolchildren. It draws circles, imitating the labyrinth and my circling back to Amherst. I will never have enough time in this house, although it will never be without me either. The deed says I own it; it actually owns me. It was there with the ten gardens, in which I learned the satisfaction of loving a patch at a time. But I didn't really learn that so much as I hope to learn it. I still hope for its habit and sometimes my days are graced by the habit of circling.

Our three kids were raised there and had their Bar and Bat Mitzvahs in the meadow (my husband is Jewish), along with a baseball game at each of their ceremonies. They never would weed the big garden. I used to argue that they had to do ten pulls a day, but they never did. Instead, they gathered eggs or milked goats or got chased by the rooster. Weeding bored them. Now in their thirties, they all have gardens and grow good tomatoes themselves. After all that resistance, the ripening is nice to see. They too are specks, and this unweeded house is part of their good, beautiful speckness also.

The big plot has now been completely overtaken by comfrey, which apparently only disappears if pigs eat it. The swamp is filled with purple loose strife, and if I didn't pay that moonlighting cop from Springfield a hundred dollars every fall to plow the swamp back, there would be no meadow. The labyrinth is long gone. Thinking about time is one way to paint our speckness on our hearts.

"Brownie," from whom we bought the place for $195,000 back in 1992, took the train up from New York City. The train left him at the bottom of the meadow near the stream. He was the book editor for the *New York Times*, and the farm had been in his family for two generations. He also moved to the city for work. Right after he retired and moved to Amherst for good, his wife died. Then he had a stroke. He had to hire a full-time gardener named Ben to do what his family had done. Ben was the best gardener I ever knew. He now lives on the streets of Northampton, with a wild look in his eye. He doesn't know me anymore, but I know him. I also know what he meant to Brownie and what Brownie meant to him.

I have the Brown family sign in my New York City garden: "Brown's Perennials." I'll take it back up when I retire. Asparagus may be a perennial. Families may be perennials. And each of us is just one part of the nineteen rooms of a good house, if we are lucky.

We drive up now instead of taking the train. And we hope Brownie never sees what we have done to the place.

In Amherst the main discussion is often what to have for dinner and whether to be a vegan, a vegetarian, or a pescatarian. Where I work, the issue is less what to eat than whether eating will be possible. To say that Amherst is all white is to ignore the several Chinese restaurants in town or the sequestered great university to our north. Otherwise, accuracy prevails.

What happens to the sense of place when work is in one place and living another? A long commute, that's what: unless you learn to grow vegetables and people at the same time. I stay busy because I choose to be both a city mouse and a country mouse. Other people can make better choices about where to place their speck. I can't. But making choices about home and place are essential to living in time, rather than living with time as your tease and trouble. I can't tell you how privileged I know I am. When you get to know a place—like where the radio stations shift or in what season the asparagus arrives—you are less tempted to wear the badge of busyness. You don't need to protect yourself from the passage of time. Time passes and you swim in it.

HOME FOR THE HOLIDAYS

There are lots of reasons for the trouble we have in time. We have split our specknesss into many pieces, making ourselves even smaller. Again, the artist deep within God and within us can help.

Most of us travel "home" for the holidays. Why? Because there is no place like home. But if your family is filled with divorces, you might have a niece with three parents to visit, a son with three parents to visit, another son with four, a ninety-year-old mother who lives half the year with one of your siblings and the other half with another. Home may be like no other—and it can find us on the road at the holidays. We will not only have portable water with us, we will have suitcases. We will pack and unpack as a holiday ritual. Like turtles, we'll wear our houses on our backs. There is nothing right or wrong about this kind of motion and its near constancy; what's troubling is when we internalize a desire to stay put while living a life on the move. Our folk wisdoms jar with each other. They cause a time and space problem, which is the unique name for contemporary stress. The word *stress* doesn't do justice to the sense of not being in the right place at the right time. It is larger than stress: It is the absence of peace. We feel that absence of peace most acutely at the holidays, but it is the longing that troubles us about time. We want to be in the right place at the right time, and we rarely are.

Environmental wisdom understands the value of both local place and global place. Sometimes we nickname this wisdom the *glocal*. We know we need both. And some of the cultural source for the time famine is in the great diversification and mobility of populations that the twenty-first century has delightfully brought to us.

Oddly, the water ritual of baptism is a place where we can find the local and the global integrated. We are baptized into a particular local water. The water may even be polluted, as Steve Thorngate notes in a 2014 *Christian Century* article. He and his wife walk along the Chicago River, a marvel of muck as well as a marvel of technology. Once dirty, it is now (sort of) clean. Thorngate tells us that he was baptized in his pastor's swimming pool. He brings us to a theology of baptism that is glocal: Baptism joins us to a particular community and a universal one at the same time. We belong not only to God but also to our place of origin. We belong not only to God but also to the whole earth. Being in one place, while knowing you are a child of God, is a lot of fun. It is frothy. You are both/and. You are as good as a turtle and can carry your peace place with you. It may not sound very complimentary to call a human a turtle—but that's only if you are out of synch with your speck and imagine yourself larger, not smaller.

Downton Abbey may help. In *Downton*, the lead character is the house. The story also unites upstairs and downstairs, in a way similar to the way baptism unites the local and the global.

Anyone who looks deeply enough at his or her own life will find that this earth of a house and this house of an earth is the lead character in their lives, too. It matters where we come from. It matters how we treat the whole. What is said in the garage does not stay in the garage, as much as we might hope for that kind of privacy and its painful disconnection. You can't just parachute in to your glocal home, nor can you just call it in. Finally, whether you want to or not, like it or not, you live in the house, with all the others. We are not stuck in one place. We are placed in one place. We are specked to one place. We have a place where we belong. We can come and go from it, for sure. But we are all students with advanced placement in homing and homelessness.

Voters increasingly want to elect people with deep local roots, people who were born and raised in their constituency. They don't want parachutists to represent them. They want the bird that has found its branch, the barnacle that has found its boat. To declare that expectation unreasonable is, of course, unreasonable. Longing persists. The fact that very few of us live in one place or are from one place is another matter entirely.

Place is an abstraction, a template that can be dropped over any point on the earth's surface. Place is also essential to art. You can't do everything, but you can do something. Place is also particular, transferable, something to which it is possible to belong. It's a feeling to the bones. And it is increasingly less likely to be our human experience.

Perhaps the longing for peaceful place comes from the original migration we made as an American people. Are we possibly still grieving that original migration in our hunger for more time? Or, more perversely, do we have a remnant of guilt for taking land from the indigenous peoples? Or is there something about the pilgrim people that isn't quite comfortable for real people, the ones who desperately want rootedness? I don't pretend to have an answer. I do know that motion bothers people and causes them to wish they were elsewhere. I learned long ago that when I am at home I want to travel and when I am traveling I want to be home. I have given my sense of place a doubleness. My doubleness is more peaceful to me than either of the parts.

Figuring out whether you want to move or not move, stay put or not stay put, really matters. It is spiritual survival for your speck. As small as a speck may be, it still has the gift and the right to name what kind of speck it is.

The other aesthetic part of being a speck is knowing how to lose what you love. Loss is inevitable. Loss happens for many of us. One-third of us have to move into a home that is not ours, for any of a number of reasons. Many artists say that they find the sculpture is complete once they get rid of everything that is not supposed to be there. Aesthetically, many of us will often have a better life if we too stop wanting a larger or more complex or different one.

Even if we aren't gardeners or sculptors, we grow and sculpt things in the earth of a certain place, in the *placeness* of a certain place, even if it is a third-floor walk-up. It is no accident that most people want to die at home. They also want to live at home, *in* a home. The luckiest gardeners die with their gloves on. The unlucky gardener has to say good-bye to the wandering Jews retrieved from Miami one winter or the inherited purple lupine or the asparagus the summer tenants tried to kill. The unlucky sculptor can't figure out what to lose and never completes his or her work.

What follows is a way to move away from the garden—to assisted living or the rehab center or the mother-in-law apartment in the kids' house—without losing the dirt in your fingernails or the soil in your soul.

People misunderstand gardeners. They think we are like normal people and resist aging and loss and what Robert Frost calls "the diminished thing." We are not. We may have all those feelings going on, but we also have another one: It is the gardener's gene and genius. What will happen to the morning glories? They may be perennial, but what if the new owners forget to water them two years in a row? We may know that we have an end, but we don't think the morning glories should also die.

I have left many gardens. What I have learned is that you don't really leave a garden. It stays with you, whether it is outside the door or not. Loss is a thief of time. Big losses steal time in a big way. Every second we live in regret is a successful heist of our place and of ourselves in time and time in place.

Specks lose small things, like a dead plant. Species, which are collections of specks, lose big things. Alan Weisman's *The World without Us* tells the story of what would happen if humans were gone, leaving small growths coming out of the top of skyscrapers. All that is left is plastic and radiation. I am thinking cell phone batteries would survive, too. His book is fired by the question of how colossal or recoverable is the damage. Like Rachel Carson's *Silent Spring*, it looks at what we have already done. Who can forget that Carson opens her book with a description of the morning, silent because the birds are gone, a casualty of the pesticides?

Anyone who wants to deeply acknowledge these griefs is writing a tragedy as their aesthetic contribution. We have lost a lot. We will lose a lot more. Good tragedy turns trouble into something beautiful and true and understood. We do grieve things. But time is not made for just grief. Time is made for the joy beyond the grief, the beauty beyond the suffering, the sense of carefree that follows too much caring.

THE PLACE WHERE THE SPECK
ACCEPTS ITS SPECKNESS

How do you keep from being gaslit, or allowing yourself to be gaslit? How do you live beyond the water bottle and its portability? How do you live well as a speck inside a species inside time and place? How do you live enough truth to become beautiful?

Instead of the badge of busyness, use the badge of place. Find words to define all that surrounds you. Make the words as beautiful as they can be. Write tragedies and comedies. Paint pictures everywhere you go. Sculpt your days. Live in the water as a part of the water. Appreciate its flow; it is also your flow. You are part of the great sacrament of the water and how it comes and goes. Do whatever you do because you want to, not because you want to change something. Be whoever you want to be, because that's who you really are.

Chapter Ten

Facing Facts as We Face God

Is it important to know God now, or can that wait? In chapter 4 I argued that life is about coming face to face or becoming intimate with God, or at least getting as close as we can get to whatever is most important to us. Many of us refuse intimacy with just about everyone. We often are not clear about what is most important to us.

At the same time, we don't know how *not* to trust the universe. The reason we sense we are so often out of time—or having bad timing instead of good timing—is that we are not clear about what truly matters.

I also argued in chapter 4 that we dare not rush to the *how* when it comes to clarity about our ultimate goal. My son, who is a great ultimate Frisbee player, often says he plays "penultimate Frisbee"; he'd like to be better than he is. When it comes to the big stuff, like God or God's face, or even the facts of which thing or person matters more than another thing or person, many of us play the big game of life penultimately. We are scared of the size of the ultimate—and we should be! How could something as important as the final point or value of our speckness not bring us, early and often, to our knees?

Here I travel a few paths to getting clear about what we need to face or give our ultimate attention to. Facing means granting a real look. It means really seeing and really being seen. It is as primary as the way a parent and child stare into each other's eyes and as primary as the way we look at our beloved as he or she passes. Learning how to really see and how to really be seen involves the eyes of the face. We only have two eyes and one face. They are more than our signature: They are us.

THE GAME OF THRONES

It is not an accident that *Game of Thrones* is an American television series set on the fictional continents of Westeros and Essos. In the first round there is a civil war, in the second there is an effort to reclaim the throne by the former realm's ruling dynasty, and the third tells about the rising threat of the impending winter and the legendary creatures and fierce peoples of the north. Each competes to be its own throne and none can qualify.

You don't have to like fantasy or water cooler conversation to enjoy the title of this award-winning series; you can just like its title and use it for your exploration of what is important. I've been arguing that it is the battle between God and Mammon that causes the time famine. We try to serve two thrones, but we run out of time, and the less important squeezes out the more important. We are often in a game of thrones, trying to throne the right thing but getting into an internal civil war. Why not make that internal civil war a great fantasy series? We play it day by day, week by week. It goes in and out of seasons. The more playful we can be about our imperfection and our competing masters, the better. In some seasons we will do better than in others. Even if we get to what might be the final season, we find ourselves up against the cold and weird creatures from the north. They may be inside of us as well as on TV.

If we have a little humor around facing God or what is most important to us, it will help. The whole structure of belief in any one God is a marvelous defense system against actually finding our way to the biggest and best. I am not suggesting you find God and then just stick to some belief system or another. I am suggesting that you keep your eyes open and your face eager for the divine, which is larger than any of the belief systems that carry God talk. There is a difference. In the one you are religious. You become a religious person, as I am, and move consensually into a system (or more than one system) that gives you a community and an ancient text in which to reside. In the other you are spiritual. By that I mean what the psalmist groaned for in wanting to see God face to face. I mean what the blessing says when it advises us to ask for God to lift up a countenance upon us. You can be both spiritual and religious. But if you can only be spiritual, by all means ache for the face of God on a regular basis. Get clear about what matters most to you and stay alert for it.

Some indigo buntings made a nest in one of our old birdhouses about five years ago. The cat got one of the babies, but we didn't know what happened to the other baby. We knew there were two eggs. We knew both hatched. We knew the gorgeous blue birds returned to feed the babies. But we never really got the whole story, so busy were we pulling weeds or doing dishes or commuting back and forth to New York. Besides, it was very hard to see inside the birdhouse, and we didn't want to disturb the babies. Yesterday we saw the indigo buntings again. This morning I saw them bring food into the birdhouse, which we had moved far away from the house and pretty much forgotten about. The thrill was enormous. It gladdened our hearts. Why? There was something important about our noticing the birds. There was something great about their surviving on our little edge of the large forest. Was it something spiritual? Or religious? Not really. What happened is this: We took the time to notice. Taking the time to notice is a prelude to facing God or the throne we have chosen to observe.

I don't want us to rush to the *how* when it comes to the big *what*. I do want us to be clear about the importance of trying. Here follow five ridiculously simple ways to face God:

1. Never get so busy that you can't enjoy a sacramental interruption. In other words, allow your clarity about what's important to always be clearing the way for what might be there, like a bird that you don't want to miss.
2. Pray. Somehow, pray. That may mean meditation. It may mean actual words. It may mean writing. But say hello to the large and the beyond in a dedicated way. Maybe it is even praying your way to prayer by always dropping to your knees at five minutes to twelve in the morning or five minutes to eight in the evening. At least that will be a reminder that there is something around that is more than you and your obligations and your loves.
3. Read the psalms, a few verses a day. They will show you people who remained alert and ached for God. They will surprise you in how not religious they are. They are about the internal civil war and its resolutions in rapturous joy.
4. Talk to others about who they think God is or what is most important to them. You will be surprised at how many people are interested in this conversation. If they say, "I don't believe there is a God," listen even more attentively. For God's sake, don't try to convince them of God!
5. Play the game of thrones, for real, with yourself. Who wins your throne?

THE AESTHETIC APPROACH

Elliot Sober writes:

Two of Barcelona's architectural masterpieces are as different as different could be. The Sagrada Família, designed by Antoni Gaudí, is only a few miles from the German Pavilion, built by Mies van der Rohe. Gaudí's church is flamboyant and complex. Mies's pavilion is tranquil and simple. Mie's, the apostle of minimalist architecture, used the slogan "less is more" to express what he was after. Gaudí never said "more is more," but his buildings suggest that this is what he had in mind.

Both artists make a bet about what is best and most beautiful. So do you, even if you are not clear that you are doing it. Finally, our calendars and our checkbooks show us what matters most to us. What do yours show?

> One reaction to the contrast between Mies and Gaudí is to choose sides based on a conviction concerning what all art should be like. If all art should be simple or if all art should be complex, the choice is clear. However, both of these norms seem absurd. Isn't it obvious that some estimable art is simple and some is complex? True, there might be extremes that are beyond the pale; we are alienated by art that is far too complex and bored by art that is far too simple. However, between these two extremes there is a vast space of possibilities. Different artists have had different goals. Artists are not in the business of trying to discover the uniquely correct degree of complexity that all artworks should have.

In each of our lives, we take a stab, we place a bet, on what matters. Deciding on the degree of complexity that we want is very important, artistically as well as scientifically.

"Albert Einstein spoke for many when he said that 'it can scarcely be denied that the supreme goal of all theory is to make the irreducible basic elements as simple and as few as possible without having to surrender the adequate representation of a single datum of experience'" ("Why Is Simpler Better?"). Many of us on our nonstop search for God (because it doesn't stop and can't stop and won't stop) want a similar simplicity that respects complexity. There is actually a wonderful scientific idea that applauds our efforts to really think and really experience the depths of our lives and experiences. It is called Occam's Razor, or the principle of parsimony. This principle says that if all you can say, based on the data, is something very small, then say something even smaller. When it comes to our faith about God, maybe all we can say is maybe. So why not say maybe? Maybe there is something bigger than my calendar and checkbook—and maybe not.

Sober continues:

> One of the most famous scientific endorsements of Ockham's Razor can be found in Isaac Newton's Mathematical Principles of Natural Philosophy (1687), where he states four "Rules of Reasoning." Here are the first two:
>
> Rule I. No more causes of natural things should be admitted than are both true and sufficient to explain their phenomena. As the philosophers say: nature does nothing in vain, and more causes are in vain when fewer suffice. Nature is simple and does not indulge in the luxury of superfluous causes.
>
> Rule II. Therefore, the causes assigned to natural effects of the same kind must be, so far as possible, the same. Examples are the cause of respiration in

man and beast, or of the falling of stones in Europe and America, or of the light of a kitchen fire and the Sun, or of the reflection of light on our Earth and the planets.

Newton doesn't do much to justify these rules, but in an unpublished commentary on the book of Revelations, he says more. Here is one of his "Rules for methodizing/construing the Apocalypse":

"To choose those constructions which without straining reduce things to the greatest simplicity. The reason of this is . . . [that] truth is ever to be found in simplicity, and not in the multiplicity and confusion of things. It is the perfection of God's works that they are all done with the greatest simplicity. He [*sic*] is the God of order and not of confusion. And therefore as they that would understand the frame of the world must endeavor to reduce their knowledge to all possible simplicity, so it must be in seeking to understand these visions. . . ."

Newton thinks that preferring simpler theories makes sense, whether the task is to interpret the Bible or to discover the laws of physics. Ockham's Razor is right on both counts because the Universe was created by God.

When it comes to artistic or scientific doors to the ultimate meanings of life, parsimony can prevail. Your clarity need not be grand. If anything, the smaller the clarity the more delightful it might be.

HUMOR AS A DOOR TO CLARITY

As John Audubon said it so well, if there is a battle between the book and the birds, always trust the birds. If you think God is hiding or you are hiding from God, consider the possibility that God is more like Br'er Rabbit or Bugs Bunny. Consider humor as a salve to put on your serious push toward certainty. Use animals when humans just won't do.

According to James H. Cone, "The role of the rabbit [in many American folk tales] is similar to that of the hare in African folk narratives—that of the trickster who shrewdly outwits and gains a victory over some physically stronger or more powerful adversary. The animal tales told by slaves with Br'er Rabbit as the hero had a meaning far deeper than mere entertainment. The rabbit actually symbolized the slave himself. Whenever the rabbit succeeded in proving himself smarter than another animal the slave rejoiced secretly, imagining himself smarter than his master" (*God of the Oppressed*). Often what matters most to us is hidden in plain sight. It may involve getting over or through evil or oppression, whether small or large. It may involve tricking our bosses. It may involve loving our bosses. What is also hidden in plain sight from most of us, but not from nature, is that we are smarter than our masters. In our own personal game of thrones, we are often being outwitted by things that master us. The game of humor allows us to outwit them.

The present-day animated version of Br'er Rabbit is, of course, Bugs Bunny, the cartoon figure created by Warner Brothers in 1940 and famously voiced by Mel Blanc. I grew up watching Bugs Bunny cartoons. Saturday mornings were filled with his antics that made me laugh as a child. I haven't watched these cartoons for a long time, but I know I would giggle if I saw him. He has ancient wisdom in a modern swagger.

Maybe God hides in Jesus so the devil can't find him. I don't know, but that helps me get one picture of the Resurrection down: Hidden in plain sight, unseen by the disciples until he was gone. Again, is it important to try to know God now or can that wait?

Fear of missing out—FOMO—is a new disease. Those of us who have lost our cell phones understand: What if something important happened and we missed it? We might ask the same question about our capacity to face God and face facts. Maybe Jesus is hiding on our cell phone. Usually when we think we have lost our phones we discover that they are actually hidden in plain sight. If Bugs were around today, you can bet he'd be stealing our cell phones.

Humor is the capacity to see what is really happening. It is seeing a little deeper than the happening dimension into the *really* happening dimension. The great Buddhist monk Thich Nhat Hanh titles one of his books *No Mud, No Lotus*, which I mentioned earlier as a great folk saying for Easter. This saying means that there is stuff happening inside the mud that is beautiful. It is a resurrection claim. It is also asking us to look at the opaque.

Some people know how to read mud and others don't. Some people even see mud as opaque, that great word that is the opposite of transparent. Thich Nhat Hanh and many other Buddhists use reading mud as a slogan for the human incapacity to ever get things completely right. We live in a kind of mud; we are at our best when we "read" it. They do so because they know how the lotus flower grows. The lotus flower is inside the mud, like a body in a tomb, ready to burst when it is ready to burst. No mud, no lotus. The lotus is hidden in plain sight in the mud. The power of the slave is hidden in his tricky humor.

Some people see what is hidden in plain sight and others don't. Cleopas saw. There are several stories told in the New Testament about the Resurrection and how it was made real to people. In each of them the God in Jesus wears a disguise. Mary thinks he is a gardener. Thomas demands to see his scars. Jesus uses the flimsy evidence of a breakfast with a broiled fish. God comes disguised so often that you have to think of him as playing hide-and-seek with humanity. But you have to figure out who is doing the hiding—us or Jesus. Most of us have had enough therapy to know that when we think our intimates are in hiding from us, we often discover that we are also in hiding from them. When it comes to wanting to see God face to face, Bugs

Bunny is not a bad guide. Like the claims of the Buddhist wisdom or the Christian wisdom, a whole lot of tricky stuff is going on in plain sight.

The story of that walk along the Emmaus Road in Luke's gospel disguises Jesus as a fellow traveler: first just any old wanderer, then a man who doesn't seem to know all the big stuff that has just happened, then a man who ought somehow to be included in supper just because it's getting dark outside. And then comes the realization, the recognition: The one we thought was dead is here. The one we thought was lost has found us.

I ran into one of our long-time members at Grand Central Station one day. She was on her way to one meeting; I, to another. I was strangely warmed by our brief visit. I didn't really want either of us to arrive at our separate destinations, so much fun was it to walk down the avenue together. We weren't going to Emmaus. But we loved the surprise of our chance meeting. We had been together the night her beloved husband died. We knew he was on his way. I had bedded down in the waiting room of the hospital to wait it out. She came to get me after he passed. We drove together through the dark Manhattan streets to take her home. All of those memories, their great grief and our intimacy in them, met in our chance encounter these several years later. She gave her husband's stamp collection to my husband. We know the rising and the falling. And now we have the sacrament of giving gifts, even during the end times, the last seasons.

On the road to Emmaus, only one of the wanderers is named: Cleopas. Some think his companion is his wife; some think it might be Luke himself. We don't know. We know nothing about either of them except that they are followers of Jesus and that they are obviously well known to the disciples. And there they are, walking along this road, utterly dejected, their lives turned upside-down, their hopes for the future dead and buried with this man Jesus—and a stranger appears beside them.

This theme of recognition is repeated throughout the Christian Resurrection stories. Mary doesn't recognize Jesus when he appears to her in the garden. It is quite possible that we wouldn't recognize Jesus either, even if he were hidden among us in plain sight, or in the mud of the tomb birthing the rising of the lotus. In our search for clarity about God, we stand in good company with slaves, rabbits, and the disciples. Very few know what is really going on. Most are tricked and tricking, very muddy but unbowed. When it comes to clarity, looking deeply into reality may find us God.

If I were a comedian, I would not leave the subject of the cell phone for long. Some days it seems to me that everybody in my front yard, Washington Square Park, is looking for his or her cell phone. Tourists are often the most comical, looking madly for the address of a cupcake shop they have heard about. When people get up from the benches in the park, they usually turn back a moment or two after leaving, checking to make sure they have their cell phones in their pockets. They then pat all their pockets, reminding me ever so much of that book *Pat the Bunny*, and with a relieved look, check one more time to make sure they haven't left anything behind before moving on. The novel I'd like to write would be *The Case of the Lost Cell Phone*, because I rarely watch anyone these days leaving a place without assuring themselves three or four times that they have their cell phones on them. Many people say that FOMO makes us more attentive to our phones: We assume that if we check our cell phones regularly—like most NYU students do up and down West Third and Fourth all day long—we won't miss out. So we stay hooked in. The students run into each other, clashing cell phones when they bump. They knock over old ladies, the few brave ones who make the mistake of walking near NYU. They also knock over the tourists, who may or may not be a casualty of their own lack of attention to their surroundings or their seasons. Many of us think that if we can just find our cell phones we can find just about anything we need. If we lose our phones, we have an emergency, a genuine, first-class emergency. We would miss out. We wouldn't just fear missing out; we would actually miss out.

The lost cell phone is nothing compared to losing a friend and not being able to find him or her, or losing a past and not being able to find it. Lost cell phones are comic metaphors for tragic matters. Most of us have lost something that we can't get back. Maybe it was our spiritual address book. Where are we, anyway, on our own road to Emmaus? How abandoned do we feel? Or maybe it was our spiritual GPS. Where are we now and what are we doing here, anyway? How did we get here—or how can we get out of here? If losing our cell phones causes us such consternation, what if we were to die and realize we had missed out on God, too?

If you have lost more than your cell phone, or even if you have lost your way and think all you have is mud, permit me a few clues as to where you might find what is lost. Each involves your looking for your cell phone in your pocket, the place we usually find it after we experience the terror that we might have lost it. Each involves recognizing someone walking with you right now. Each of them involves trusting the mud and its lotus bearing urgency.

Clue One: Watch how trouble hides. We all know it is there but decide to not look at it. The great business strategist Peter Drucker argues that culture eats strategy for breakfast. How can you know if you live in a sick office culture? Hear these loud clues. They constitute the wrong time wrong place culture that creates bad timing.

Important things are said in the parking lot, not in meetings.
People talk about each other, not to each other.
Everything is understood transactionally or politically: If I say this she'll do that, so I won't.
You don't respect the other people; you manipulate them.

You count every week the number of times you hear yourself saying, "I couldn't say that."

Clue Two: If you are in a marriage or a partnership or a family where hidden realities are often obscured in the mud, hear them. Hear the realities of the mud. Recognize the mud. Tell the person walking beside you about the mud. What do you have to lose that you haven't already lost?

Clue Three: If you see a beautiful building or temple, like the Sagrada Família, don't wonder for long about how expensive it was to build or how long it took to build. Remember those who built it. The ones who mixed the concrete. The ones who signed the checks. Honor work and workers.

Clue Four: Remember that the Occupy Movement was birthed in a slogan that everybody understood. The slogan went out by e-mail from Canada: "Occupy Wall Street, Bring Tents." Recognize that you get it, and hang on to your tent. One e-mail birthed an entire movement. You'd almost think Bugs Bunny was afoot.

Clue Five: Befriend your own personal tragedy. Recognize it. You can't be unraped, but you can live after rape. One out of three American women does. Why not you? Recognize the mud. And remember what Nikki Giovanni said, after she said you can't be unraped. She said: "I told everybody about how difficult my childhood was and then they started thinking I was pathetic. They had no idea what a happy childhood I had anyway." Recognize the mud for its birthing qualities, which are your birthing qualities.

Clue Six: In his now-famous book *Between the World and Me*, Ta-Nehisi Coates writes elegiacally about his fears for his son. We didn't need Coates to tell us that his son wasn't safe. We didn't need so many shootings to tell us that certain kinds of people are powerfully less safe than others. We did need Black Lives Matter to put a megaphone on the mud that disproportionately harms. That megaphone births a lotus. It is a resurrection, sprung right from the mud of dehumanization. The misery was hidden in plain sight. So is the joy.

David Harris Gerson writes:

> One of the most powerful moments during my reading of *Between the World and Me* by Ta-Nehisi Coates was when he expressed a similar sentiment. There he was, a young father, when a black man he knew from college, a devout man named Prince Jones, was murdered by police. The murder shook him, and while at the funeral, as people around him called to forgive the offending officer, as people focused on this one cop, Coates was unmoved: "The need to forgive the officer would not have moved me, because even then, in some inchoate form, I knew that Prince was not killed by a single officer so much as he was murdered by his country and all the fears that have marked it from birth. . . . Forgiving the killer of Prince Jones would have seemed irrelevant to me. The killer was the direct expression of all his country's beliefs. For the crime of destroying the body of Prince ones, I did not believe in forgive-

ness. When the assembled mourners bowed their heads in prayer, I was divided from them because I believed that the void would not answer back."
("The Origin of 'Scapegoat'")

Sometimes the only resurrection that is possible is facing the void. Just face it. Don't work yourself up into lather about how much faith you have lost because of how much harm has been done to you or yours. Just face the mud. Often people say to me when I get overeager about my activism, "Donna, calm down. We just need you to stand in the mud with us." Aha.

Clue Seven: The solution to your time famine and my time famine, also hidden in plain sight, is not more down time or vacation or even rest. The solution to the time famine is to choose between God and Mammon, between wholeheartedness and the divided self.

Sometimes I get sick of my own clues. They expand and expand. They have no simplicity to them. I think of myself as providing nothing but hints from a spiritual Heloise. I can't tell you that any of these clues will help you find the hidden clarity I claim is there in the mud and the muck. I have no money-back guarantees.

All of these clues, simple as they are, relate to great complexity. There are tons of ways to get lost and tons of ways to find and be found. Starting wherever you are, even if your cell phone is lost, is the most important clue. Finding the humor in the absurdity of any given situation will go a long way to taming it, and you. Once tamed, you can go wild for God.

Someone wise said that God is most like a parent who throws you up in the air and then catches you. God catches us. Another wise person corrected that odd folk wisdom about how God won't send you more than you can bear. That's not really true. God does send some people more than they can bear. But God won't give you more than your community can bear—or so we have to hope. God hangs around, hidden in plain sight.

Let me say one more thing about the hidden God. God is hidden in nature, always right there, always being raped, always wondering why we don't love the mess as much as we could. God is hidden in nature and not just in our relationships to each other, important as they are. I am pretty sure God is most hidden in plain sight in the seasons, the energy cycles of the cosmos, the living channels of energy that pump our blood and our water, the dandelions that resurrect their puffballs every year.

Will that God give you the clarity you need to center yourself in such a way as to permit your being off center? I don't know. I do know that many people have followed the roads of art and science and humor—and ultimate Frisbee—to find their way. You might also. My only certainty is that you may and should and can try. Face the facts. Face God. Face yourself. Face all three, one at a time.

Chapter Eleven

That Pesky First World Problem

I used to think that the real drag on my time was that I both wanted to do good and live well. Part of me wanted to connect to social justice and change the dynamics of the world, and the other part of me wanted to enjoy my privilege. My privilege was both freedom and material wealth. Compared to the rest of the world, I am right at the top. I probably won't get deported. I probably won't get shot. I am an unlikely candidate for oppression. My country probably won't erupt, as Syria has, into a civil war so great that I will have to put my children in small boats and take them to unknown locations. I probably won't have to rely on the hospitality of the Canadians or the Danes or the Germans.

And yet, and still, I do not *not* care about the people in these diverse boats. I do care. I am riven. Warren, who reads the *New York Times* religiously every morning, pointed out to me the other week that on Wednesday of 2016 the *Times* used the word riven in four articles. (They are listed at the end of the book if you want to be bothered by them, as we were.) I am not sure I needed the *Times*'s confirmation of my experience, but I knew I was seeing a lot of people who felt riven or cut in two. I also realized that *riven* is my middle name: Doing good and living well are expensive! They are especially expensive in terms of time.

Riven means being torn in two, rent asunder, split apart. It describes well the cross down my middle. I want to have both God and Mammon, both self and other. And I fail at that unity almost every day, all day long. It roots my own bad timing in a kind of sin, that of missing the mark of my full humanity. And I am not alone: Many people I know experience the same splits. They eat away at us. And who are we to complain about being eaten away, when many don't even eat?

What follows here are ways to become more complete. Not fully complete, but more unified, more whole. It is particularly for the privileged, like me, who are riven. I never have enough of me to go around, even for me and also for them. I no longer think of these matters as either good or bad, but instead as givens. They operate on another, more psychological and spiritual frame as well as the moral frame. They are matters of being human and being incomplete humans, who long for completion.

JESUS: A MOVING TARGET

Jesus says if you can see him in someone else you can see him: "They [the disciples] also will answer, 'Lord, when did we see you hungry or thirsty or a stranger or needing clothes or sick or in prison, and did not help you?' He will reply, 'Truly I tell you, whatever you did not do for one of the least of these, you did not do for me'" (Mt 25:44–46). He has long made this allegiance with the stranger his hallmark.

Meet Myrna. The United States government deported Myrna a while back, and recently she walked to the border and was allowed to walk across the border and meet her fourteen-year-old and eight-year-old daughters, who were also brought there. Rev. Juan Carlos Ruiz of the New York City Sanctuary Coalition walked in both directions with the daughters and the mother, across the border and back across. We all see Jesus in this successful reunion. It was my privilege to speak with a man at border control and to urge him to allow the passage to take hold. He did not agree on the phone to allow the passage, but rumor has it that he did. Myrna will now apply for refugee status, and we believe she will be so granted. She spoke to our congregation on Pentecost and spoke in her own language, so that we could try to hear her across the divide of our English and her Spanish. It was an awkward experience, to put it mildly. One older gent walked out, grumbling, "I don't understand what she is saying."

It is easy to identify with Jesus the successful companion. I also want to comment on his spotty track record. For every one glorious reunification, there are thousands that never happen. Jesus remains unseen, just like most of us remain incomplete. We want these coming togethers to happen over and over again, but they don't. And we don't know how to improve on our track records. We grumble on our way out of service: "I just don't understand what she is saying." Besides, how could I possibly help?

My favorite refugee story comes from Sarajevo. Remember Sarajevo? One of the women who walked out of her native land during that crisis took a small suitcase with her Sabbath candles and lace tablecloth in it. Her son wrote about his picnics with his mom in the camps, saying that they had less food than other people, until she brought out her tablecloth and candles. Then people shared with them. "Bread and Roses" is the title of the story he told.

His mom gathered people together and put them back together around a tablecloth and candles. They always shared their food with her. The son stopped complaining about what she had brought along for their journey.

Unfortunately the tablecloth got dirty. They had to sell the candlesticks and ran out of candles fairly early. For every one refugee who gets out and up, there are thousands, if not millions, who do not. What are we to do with their Jesus and his spotty track record?

We are to learn how to be riven until the spirit fully lights on us and in us. We are incomplete, just as Jesus declares he is. He doesn't say anything about right and wrong but instead says that he is incomplete. He needs the stranger to be seen. He needs the stranger to be fully understood.

Many of us describe Jesus as the true human or the ideal human. If he is riven and split, so are we. Learning to be riven is a practical art. It is the decision to intend to become whole and to know we will die in parts. It is the self-direction of touching suffering and learning to be less afraid of it. La-Shawn Warren of the New Jersey Institute for Social Justice says, "I have come to realize it is impossible to change the world without being proximate to the brokenness we seek to heal" ("A Christian in Public and Private").

Likewise, in the Pentecost story the people all had only their own language. They were jammed together in an upper room. Suddenly, a spirit came upon them and they experienced the miracle of understanding each other. They became whole and complete after being partial and incomplete. They understood each other and recognized themselves in each other.

The most practical thing I can tell you about becoming whole and complete is here: Stay close to suffering. Approximate it. Don't be afraid to touch the people you can't help. Learn to be as useless as they are. As my friends told me last year during a Black Lives Matter event, where I was feeling particularly hopeless and helpless: We just need someone to stand in the mud with us. That pesky mud returns. Surprisingly, many of us put a lot of effort into avoiding suffering: "Don't go to that neighborhood" or "Don't go to that school" or "Be safe." Slight turns in the direction of touching suffering can change these behaviors. Go to that neighborhood or that school. Accompany an immigrant to an ICE check-in. Tutor. Make sure you don't live your life protected from suffering. You will only become more riven, more isolated, more alone. You will certainly become less complete, and that lack of completion will dog your days and your ways. Becoming proximate to brokenness will actually make you less open. I don't know how that works so much as I know it does.

In horrifying situations, like that being experienced around the world by the Syrian refugees, you can at least grant the courtesy of noticing the plight of the wanderers. That noticing makes a difference, for you and for them. Of course, those wandering right now—no matter when *right now* is, wonder as they wander. Does anybody give a damn that I am here right now, far from home, not knowing where my feet will take me? The answer can be, impotently, yes: especially for those on whom the spirit does light and who have spiritual gumption.

Lots of people say they are burned out, using an unfortunate automotive metaphor. My argument here is that the truth is different. Most of us aren't even lit. How could we burn out?

Complete humanity is a destination we covet, biologically as well as spiritually. Spirit-filled people have the capaciousness for brokenness that the unspirited or dispirited do not. Why not be spirit filled? The spirit is willing on just about any occasion.

FINDING YOUR OWN PILGRIM, YOUR INNER REFUGEE, YOUR OWN IMMIGRANT

My denomination, the United Church of Christ, has an unfortunate habit of calling every other church Plymouth or Pilgrim Church. We imagine ourselves as *pilgrims*, which is a much nicer word than *refugee* or *immigrant*. The latter implies something wrong about you or yours or your homeland; the former implies that you are marching in the light of God. I love the United Church of Christ. I love the United States of America. I am torn, even riven, by the way we blame immigrants and deport them regularly. I fear that we are making a lie out of our own welcoming and open truth. We are becoming a forgery of ourselves. We are lying to ourselves about ourselves. These forgeries are at the root of our sense of bad timing or time famine. Consider this poem about pilgrims by William Stafford:

> They come to the door, usually carrying or leading
> a child, always with The Book held between them
> and the world. They quote Ezekiel, Daniel, Kings.
> They look at us and think of Nebuchadnezzar
> eating the grass. It is good to listen, because
> maybe they are angels, and behind them the sky arches,
> the trees glisten in worship of the sun.
> These travelers in the Word and their offspring have
> their commission from somewhere, filtered down, through
> mistakes, pride, greed, and the plans committees
> make, the way pilgrims have always come.
> Over their shoulders day extends its hand;
> beside them a child whimpers. It bows its head
> as we bow: it hungers; it cries; it will be fed.

It is about the visit at the door of those who would convince us of something. I want to think of all of us—insiders and outsiders, first- and second- and third-worlders—as having something to offer to each other. We are all angels to each other. We can complete each other. We are all both hosts and guests.

Getting a hold of our own metaphors about ourselves will help heal our bad timing and turn it into good timing. How? By decreasing the attention we have to pay to our forgeries and allowing us to walk in more truth.

Consider another metaphor beyond the pilgrim one. Think of how we look at the English settlement in Virginia in 1607. It is a prime story about how we Americans think of our wandering suffering. We were also immigrants, and we have turned our wandering into heroism about ourselves. Maybe there was also terrible suffering. Have we come through that suffering, or just ignored it? Have we come through the suffering we have inflicted on others? How much did our first world lives, such as they are, come from theft of land from the indigenous and theft of labor from the slaves? What is it that we are really hiding? I have had to look at my own privilege through the lens of how much it actually cost others and came from others. I have a fundamental incompletion here. There are no possible reparations that are adequate. But I can notice. I can acknowledge the riven. I can even see the separation of peoples as fundamental, not accidental, to my existence.

What practical suggestion lurks here? Either extend the title pilgrim to everyone or call yourself a refugee—or both. Know what you want to say when you knock on another's door. You do have something to say and to offer. Be ready to listen to the angels who knock on your doors. Above all, stop denying history and forging your truth. It will help as you try to become complete and try to have enough time.

It grounds us in a beginning. What does the beginning have to do with today? What does history have to do with us? Lots. But we have to take the time—the time we *do* have—to develop the capacity to understand our origins. Why bother caring about anything besides yourself, or about anything that is not yourself? Why bother caring about the long ago? Because without that care for the proximate, you are split in two. You are riven. Is there anything you can do to help? Yes: you can notice. That may be all you can do, but at least you can do that. The most interesting people are the people in the corners. The most interesting people are the ones you can't see. They are hidden in plain sight.

There is a great way of reading parables in which you take the role of everything in the parable. You are both the prodigal son and the father and the brother. Why not learn to read American history from the point of view of all the people in the story? Why not become complete?

You will have better timing and enough time if you can see the other. You might even see Jesus. You might become more capable of being whole or truly human.

LOANING MONEY TO FRIENDS AS FOREIGNERS
AND FOREIGNERS AS FRIENDS

A final possibility in time management and care for the first-worlder is here: Why not give your money and matter away? Why not even things out? Or, if you can't part from your money—either because there isn't enough or you don't care to—at least you can learn to open your heart to the experience of the other. You can surely make it your aim to be complete and to befriend the other. That befriending is much more important than giving people money. Giving money keeps you in the power position. You don't want that; you want to equalize power. If you are proximate to the brokenness, you will find yourself wanting to give your money away. If you are far from it, you can't buy your way out of your own incompleteness. Be careful with this practical suggestion. Be very careful that it be money from the wholesome and whole-hearted heart and not from the heart so punished that it is buying its way out of misery. Of course, it can be a little of both. But as usual, the more God gets the less Mammon gets.

I just about always say no to the beggars on the streets of New York—and I always look them in the eye and ask them how they are doing. They aren't angry or disappointed. They also aren't happy. I look them in the eye for myself, not for them.

Changing your metaphor as a pilgrim or refugee can also help. It is likely that changing that metaphor will change your giving patterns. My bet is that you will find yourself more genuinely generous instead of guiltily generous. There is a huge difference. The former appreciates time; the latter wastes time.

THE MOST PRACTICAL PRACTICE
OF ALL FOR FIRST-WORLDERS

Whole cost accounting is an economic theory that asks us to look at more than price. We use it automatically when we charge our expense accounts for mileage: We don't just pay for the gas, we pay for the whole car and what it really costs to drive it, in insurance, depreciation, and repairs. It is funny that we don't pay for the earth that way, or for our time or our bridges that way. We could do whole cost accounting on our time and find enormous amounts of time just sitting there, hoping to be used.

To put it bluntly: Things cost a lot more than we think they do. Those of us who are time famished especially need to put a price on our "free" time and observe how much we are paying our job or our worries or our false metaphors or our self-forgeries.

James Baldwin says, "Anyone who has struggled with poverty knows how extremely expensive it is to be poor." Genuinely cheap people would see how expensive their servitude is and repent. We would pay for our time by not getting paid by others to buy it. The coin is not just wages or salaries; the coin of servitude is also doing what we think other people think we should do.

There is another coin, and, oddly, it is inefficiency. Some people call me the Henry Ford of spirituality (as well as politics) instead of the Martha Stewart of spirituality. I appreciate the joke. What do I know about writing? I know that you have to get away from it to get to it. You have to take a walk more often when you are on a serious deadline. We make so many mistakes when we are rushing! I have told everybody I know the story I related in an earlier chapter about the socks that had to be sent back the same day the stove knobs had to be sent back. Sending the socks to the stove company and the knobs to the socks company didn't help anybody. It ended up taking twice the time. Why did things get so out of whack? Because I was rushing. In whole cost accounting, we add up the costs of our mistakes, too.

What would it mean to have a spirited and spiritual time budget—"Every time I say yes to some obligation I don't want, I am paying twenty dollars in time," or some such enumeration? We'd account for the costs of our mistakes, the costs to our peace, the lost relaxation, and the price of antacids. We first-worlders are, above all, proud of our efficiency. We might also be shamed by our inefficiency.

THE POOR LITTLE RICH PEOPLE

First-worlders have unique problems with our bad timing. Sometimes it is truly bad, as in immoral. Other times it is incomplete, as in our active separation from others. More often it is just inefficient and we lose what we really want. You might even call us the poor little rich people. That would not be all bad; indeed, it would be a great improvement.

I have mentioned the God and Mammon conundrum frequently. The idolatry problem is the truly big one. When we are wealthy and can't let go of our wealth, we put ourselves in the God position. When we confuse ourselves or our own security of self with the divine, we are idolatrous. When we position God above and first, we find our openness to the other expanding. We find a way to get it right, as in right relationship to ourselves, the divine, and the other. God first takes money out of the driver's seat, and things rearrange themselves almost automatically. We find ourselves free to connect with others and free to discontent with our wealth.

Conclusion

In this book, I have shown the spiritual roots of the practical problems that surround time. I have said that the reason we don't have enough time is that we try to serve both God and Mammon at the same time. We are double-timing the divine and Mammon as well. We indulge in a harmful version of personal fraud by pretending we can do everything Mammon commands while also hitting the mark of our true humanity. We think we can be what we're meant to be, while also being what our culture wants us to be.

I have said that sin is missing the mark of our true humanity. I have not wanted to say that with judgment or blame so much as to say it as a fact: one that, if recognized, can be somewhat changed. I don't think we can or will be perfect. Instead, we can be more honest and joyful imperfectionists.

I have wanted to size up the size of our time trouble. I have relied on averages, numbers, and directions instead of completion or perfection.

I have argued that we flow through time as though swimming or floating in water. I have argued for flow instead of finish, for incompletion as opposed to completion. I have talked about how things will never get done and also that we may enjoy sleeping at night with a long to-do list. Time is like water: all around us, always, and rarely noticed or appreciated.

I have shown the way time is different for those of us who live in first world settings than it is for those who lived in former worlds or live in different worlds. Again, there is no stigma in being a first-worlder. The problem is lack of recognition about how pervasively we are first-worlders and how much of who we are has to do with our cultural and economic marching orders. We may dare march to a different drummer.

The first six chapters were spiritual and theological in nature, driving us to the *why* of our life, which is to live well in whatever time we have. The last six chapters have turned toward the practical and give what can only be called time management skills. Since these are not just skills but rather a spiritual orientation, the chapters try to dialogue with each other. The practical and the spiritual are friends, not enemies.

We are to number our days toward wisdom.

We are to not take ourselves so seriously. We are but specks in time and space. Beautiful specks, but specks nonetheless.

When we face facts—like the fact that we will die—we start to face God. We see that it is great news that we get out of the way so someone else can be born. We rejoice in our smallness and stop trying to be God—and start hitting the mark of our humanity.

As you leave this reading experience, you might agree with some or all of the analysis here about what's gone wrong and what might be right. You will probably agree with enough of it to want to make a change or two in the way you live. You might want to move out of bad timing and into good timing. You might want to feast on time. You may even jump off the high board into the water of big change. You may want a sea change not just a pond change. You may want something as big or small as a baptism into a new way of life—or better yet, a resurrection.

Either way or any way, you will need to decide the size of the change you want to make. The main suggestion of this book is to custom design your approach to your time and to make your time your own. Your own timing will be good timing; someone else's timing will be bad timing.

Here I will use the Christian understandings of baptism as an entry point into the new and the renewed. If you only make one thing new about your experience of time, that will be a victory for this writer.

You have a problem when you don't have any solutions you like. You may want to become completely new and not be able so to do. You may want small solutions to large problems—urgent incrementalism—and wonder if you have the self-discipline. Just about everybody has this kind of problem today.

BAPTISM AS A SPIRITUAL AND PRACTICAL SOLUTION

Take baptism, a newing and renewing ceremony. Keeping a high bar for baptism—the parents must join the church and promise to raise the child in Christ, and the child must attend Sunday school and confirmation class—means that people will probably say yes and act no. There is this thing called a time famine; it manifests in soccer practice on Sundays or just plain old snuggling in bed with your children.

Keeping a low bar for baptism is like planting a twenty-dollar plant in a one-dollar hole—a great phrase of Loren Mead, the founder of the Alban

Institute. You can't sprinkle spirituality or Christianity on people; it begs for immersion.

Here I want to argue for a kind of adult baptism, one with an incremental low bar that moves you toward a higher one, regularly.

In certain ways, the worst thing we can do is not decide on a low or high bar. This just keeps people confused. It is a kind of slavery, not knowing what to do so much that you do nothing, or you do something too large for yourself and your reality—and fail so spectacularly at becoming completely new that you just stop trying.

As you go through the practical exercise of discovering what you want to do next, imagine yourself as a child, one with good parents who want to do the right thing by you.

You may know the Moses story. The Hebrew slave has to give up her child. She puts him in the river's water. She actually gives him up to the water. In baptism we give our children up to the water, the great water of life. We let them go. We let them go to God. In adult baptism, we can do the same thing. We may have been baptized once and realize that we need to try again.

In the story, Pharaoh's daughter picks the baby Moses up and out of the water. Isn't it interesting that Moses, the great leader of the Hebrew People, was both a child of privilege and a child of slavery? An unlikely savior picks Moses up out of the water, only for him to go on and drown Pharaoh's army. The baby is put in the water by an innocent slave and pulled out by a family member of Pharaoh's army, the one that got drowned in the river, chasing the slaves. The Passover story is also a kind of baptism story, creating as much salvation and confusion as it can.

I am a synchretist. I see the birth canal as part of the great crossover from prelife to life. I see death as crossing another river. Water is both a sign of terror to come and salvation seen. I am also a diluter in chief. I want to figure out how to baptize children with integrity and without certainty. I want you to have practical and glorious ways to become new in your timing. I want you to own your ways and not stay hung up on other people's directions or decisions for your life.

If we make it easy to baptize children, keeping the bar low, we'll have a revolving door on our own relativism. We won't attract the intensity of the religious search of the "none of the aboves," who intensely *don't* want to be hypocritical about something as important as God and community. So they stay out, left behind in the bulrushes and orphaned by things that might help them get picked up by Pharaoh early enough to challenge him later. When orphaned and sprinkled with a little bit of this and a little bit of that, we plant their glory in holes too small for growth. Instead of being rooted, they become root-bound.

On the other hand, if we make it too hard to baptize children, people just won't do it. They'll find a simpler way. Of course, there is no simple way, but we don't have to tell them that yet.

Your inner child will be having the same rumbles as you think about what to do about yourself. God picks you up out of the water, and Mammon in the person of Pharaoh probably catches you. You won't leave Mammon behind just because you try to flow with God, as a way of becoming new. You try to get ahead of Mammon, knowing that pharaohs are everywhere.

I was baptized on the seventh day of my life. I found out later why: My Missouri Synod Lutheran tribe actually believed that if I died before I was baptized I would go to hell. I find that more than a little extreme. I have lost respect for that version of hell, the kind that condemns unbaptized children to eternal suffering. Simultaneously, I have gained respect for hell and for what baptism prevents.

I come to you as diluter in chief, ready to make a case for original sin. The knot of our baptismal theology is that we are both saints and sinners: created to head straight for glory, but all fallen. We sin when we misuse our time and try to worship both God and Mammon unsuccessfully. The sin is in lost direction. We stop aiming for our true humanity.

I will base my baptismal case in Michelle Alexander's theology and that of St. Paul, who argues that all—everyone, you and me and them—have sinned and fallen short of the glory of God. No one can become new until they realize how distant we are from glory. In *The New Jim Crow: Mass Incarceration in the Age of Colorblindness*, Alexander argues that we Americans need to get in touch with our inner criminality. She borrows heavily from the theology of James Baldwin, who tells us that he has only one accusation for his country: Get over your innocence. Baldwin and Alexander both argue that our innocence—our refusal to be wrong about anything—turns us into people who wrong. Until we acknowledge that we have done wrong with our timing and that we have known lots of bad timing, we won't get very far toward the new.

As diluter in chief—as someone who respects orthodox Christianity and knows most people don't and can't respect it—I want to tell you how my syncretism works. Truth in observance: I have three children who were named and baptized, and I had Passover with all three of them last year. I have three grandchildren, none of whom were baptized. Yes, we had a unique Seder. My daughter-in-law is a rabbi. My three baptized children are all practicing Jews, siding with their father's side of the river.

Baptism is the subject about which Christians—and interfaith families—love to fuss more than any other. The very fuss dilutes the meaning of baptism while alerting us to its importance. I am interested in what baptism really means. I am interested in the more interesting dilutions, the ones that mix us up and spit us out into the great unnavigable seas of life. I am fully respectful of the one baptism that starts us off in life—whether as infants or later—and also interested in how often we have to enter the water of renewal again.

Baptism means that even innocent children can and will be sinners. Baptism announces where that beautiful, white-ruffled, lace-dabbled baby is going: She is going to join the human race, and she will become part of the great unwashed. The water of baptism is a sign of the glory of God and that we can return again and again to glory. It is a sacrament.

A sacrament is an outward sign of an inner grace. In baptism we wash the child before he or she has had much chance to sin. Another kind of baptizer asks the child to embrace the grace of God when he or she comes of age. Or, if you are a Christian minister working at a Jewish synagogue and married to a Jew, you put in your Romemu newsletter something like this: "Come to the baby naming at the synagogue today, and all are invited to her baptism tomorrow at Advent Lutheran." This interfaith minister is a good friend of mine. She joins me in preferring dilution while knowing that immersion will be the only way to newness.

In my denomination—the UCC—today, we have a great debate going on about baptism. We have the low-bar baptism people, like me, where if somebody calls up and asks to have a baby done, we do the baby. We dilute baptism in order to make it accessible for people like me, who are multiple and multiplying in our sense of God. We also have the high-bar baptism people, who require the parents have to join the church, pay the dues and not just promise to raise the children in Christianity but sign the Sunday school roster for a dozen years. These are the baptismal concentrators and intensifiers.

The high-bar baptism people argue that Christianity is a big thing and that it takes a lifetime to learn. I agree with them here. Loren Mead is right when he says, "You can't take a twenty-dollar plant and put it in a one-dollar hole. It won't grow and it won't thrive." The gardener in me knows how important it is to dig a good hole if you want to plant something that flourishes. The high-bar baptism people have a great argument, but their argument is not realistically accessible to most people today. They don't have time to join a church, they probably won't live in the same community for very long, and they know that the F and Q trains rarely work efficiently on weekends. Plus, they are tired. As you decide your time direction, you may want to acknowledge how tired you already are in trying to become new.

At Coral Gables Congregational Church, my congregation in Miami, we had intense struggles on this matter, mostly because the gay-friendly Cubans in Miami—all six hundred of them, the ones who had left the well-dug hole of the Roman Catholic Church and wanted to raise their children in the UCC or one of its greatly diluted clones—came to us in droves asking us to baptize their babies. They had no intention of hanging around, but they wanted to dress the baby up and invite all their relatives to something that looked like the old world. Baptisms were mostly done for the *abuelas*—the grandmothers.

We developed a well-diluted compromise: We charged the families eighty dollars for the baptism—about as much as child care or soccer. They had to attend two sessions with one of the ministers and become a group and talk about their hopes for their children. They all came. They all made friends with each other, because they were all spiritually stuck in the same boat. And because they found friends who also had newborns, many of them stuck to the congregation. The baptism was relatively inconsequential. We started them at one o'clock in the four corners of the building and went until about three, often doing twelve to sixteen baby waterings per Sunday. We were the diluters in chief. We made a little opening in a closed door. We dug a little bit of the hole to make people understand that all have sinned and fallen short of the glory of God. The glory was the point, not the sin, but we weren't ignoring the sin either.

If you figure out how to pay for your newness and number the number of sessions you will devote to it, you will find yourself strangely serious about it. Our baptizing families weren't tricked straight out. But they did become a community, digging deeper holes for themselves and their children, and they did talk to each other honestly about their lives.

Quickie baptisms, like we did in Florida, are just the face of the meaning of baptism. We began the process of honest conversation; we did not complete it. Baptism's meaning is that we all will sin and fall short of the glory of God. Its meaning is that even if we become president of the United States, we will still be shackled in what we can do to make a difference. There are genuine limits on our time. They are real. We are human. I want to raise up people who know how to immerse themselves in difficulty over and over and not be afraid of it. I want what many now call resilience to prevail.

I have often joked that my diluted theology actually comes from my being a born-again pagan. I'm not kidding. I may follow a convicted felon and join the people who baptize in his name, but I am not sure Christians have the only route to God. I always wanted to give my own children a lot of protections, thus their Bar and Bat Mitzvahs as well as their baptisms. I also howl at the moon with them as often as I can. I may not know how to help it. I am fallen. I am fallen down. I also know how to get up. I am not orphaned. I have been picked up out of the water again and again, sometimes by very unlikely lifters.

Michelle Alexander also notes the sins that abound in we diluters and born again pagans. She says, in a way that chills me to my core, that the most violence happens in the most diverse nations. By that she surely means my nation. We are much more tribal than we admit. We are much more sinful than we dare to admit. We say we love diversity, but we don't know how to truly fall into it or out of it. My amazingly liberal and open congregation can't help its racist microaggressions, once suggesting to an African American Oberlin graduate that she probably finds it "hard to be around such intellectual Christians" or fussing about the slogan Black Lives Matter on a regular basis. Microaggressions? Nope, these are just tribal aggressions wearing doctorate degrees. Many of us first-worlders are seriously attached to getting *A*s on our self-improvement report cards. That is itself the kind of problem that will keep us from success at living in the world that is already new.

Can we talk about sin? Sin is falling short of the glory of God. The *glory*: the place where we are bound. You can emphasize either of Paul's lines. You can walk around yelling all have sinned or whisper about the glory of God. Lots of people do both, weakly. I'd like to do both nimbly. Self-flagellation is our favorite game. Republicans are especially interested in the sins of sex. Democrats are especially interested in the sins committed on the way to democratic pluralism. Neither are getting very far. Maybe we need to be baptized again and again as well as born again and again. Maybe we flow in water because we don't know how not to. Maybe we need to abolish the words *ought* and *should* and *must*, or at least put ourselves on a diet of five a day. I did that once, as a writer, with exclamation points. The diet really helped. Examples: We must get rid of racism or racist attitudes! We must set a high bar for baptism in order to create better Christians! We should not be so racist! We should raise our children well and dig deep holes for them in which to thrive! We should not let children use tablets! We should teach others out of our sinful tribalism! We don't know how not to yet. People who get over the time famine and into time feast know how to use the words *may* and *might* well. They translate all the above sentences, taking out the *musts* and putting in the *mays*.

At our Seder this year my six-year-old grandson and four-year-old grand-daughter got three dollars each for finding the hidden Afikomen. It is part of the ritual of the Seder, to hide it and for the grandfather to give a prize. First, showing their glory, they pooled their money, deciding they would share it. Then, showing their perfidy, they whispered to me that they were saving for an iPad. According to Caleb, "Every Jewish kid I know has an iPad." Should they have their own iPads? Perhaps at infant baptism, we should register the kids for e-mail accounts and get them cell phones. Should we? Should we not? Neither. In your time budget should you do more or less e-mail? Neither. Instead, you may make a choice about these matters.

What about more focus on what we may do and might do—like head straight for the glory of God? We won't do all that we should do. We will instead—thank you, St. Paul—fail. "The good that I would do, I do not, and the evil that I would not do, I do." We should not fail, but we will. Thank God for the refreshing waters of baptism and the promises it makes us make.

So many parents just give in to their two year olds using iPads. Why? Why not? What "should" they do? What would they do if they experienced less orphaning blame and more parenting care?

Keeping a low bar for baptism is like throwing children into the water and hoping somebody—somewhere, somehow—will pick them up and give them a chance. Baptism may look all white and frilly and innocent, but it is not. Parents know what it means to parent. We come trembling into baptism and Bar Mitzvahs.

As the diluter in chief, I'd like to put in a good word for the concentrated blessing of the holy water, the water we bless with spirit in the service, giving it spirit. Speaking as the low-bar type of Christian, permit me to acknowledge my sin and to place it where it belongs: in the ways we head for glory. We don't head for glory as plagued perfectionists. We head for glory as imperfectionists. We know we won't arrive. We stop expecting that we will be Christians, ever, and try to be Christians this afternoon.

If you want to be really chilled, consider this: What if we were wrong about religion and baptism and God and sin all along? What if all this time, trying to do good and not do wrong, we were doing wrong while trying to be good? What if all our double-timing were an absurd waste of time? What if the way through sin were to understand that we are godly but not gods, headed in God's direction but not in order to dethrone God? What if we were wrong all along, while thinking we were right? Before that chill comes, I say we sit in the glory: the glory of not knowing, the glory of not always having to be right, the glory beyond doing and being good, the glory for which we were intended from the start. It sure beats innocence.

The knot and nub of our baptism is that we are both saints and sinners, created to head straight for glory but fallen along the way into should-ing instead of could-ing. The water embraces both of these. We can all do the little thing that Pharaoh's daughter did. We can pick each other up out of the water and give each other another chance. We can refuse to be innocent about the glory of God. We can become ready for its startle and its marvel.

A RITUAL

You may like the metaphor of baptism for your newness as a person, the one who is going to have good timing, going forward. Create one! You may want to borrow from this one.

> What we have here is just water, made holy by the active Spirit of God. What we have here is just a child, but one more of many whom God could not love any more. The hairs on her/his head are numbered. When Jesus said, suffer the little children to come unto me, he meant it. In his name we are here. Your inner child is also welcome.

Ask the parents: Will each of you as parents covenant together to teach your child those meanings and mysteries that come from the rich heritage of your spiritual forebears? Will you share with him/her the love and caring that you yourselves found in parents and friends? And will you tell her/him of a people and a family larger than their home and kin to which he/she belongs and unto whom she/he is called?

Ask the godparents: Will you help them?

Ask family and friends: Will the family and friends please rise and add your blessing?

To the congregation: Please rise. Do you promise to be so active and real as the body of Christ that this child can't help but know God? If so, please respond, "We so promise." You may be seated.

Ask the parents: How is the child to be named?

The ritual is to remember your name. Baptism is about your name. Becoming new can involve a new name or remembering an old one.

LITTLE WAYS OF BECOMING NEW

Matt Cutts is a very popular TED talker. His "Try Something New for Thirty Days" is a brilliant and practical approach to the matter of becoming new. He digs a deep whole, thirty days at a time. Listen to it. I have, several times.

Based on both the baptism approach and Cutts's approach, answer these questions and decide what to do and be.

How serious is my bad timing right now?
What level of time famine do I have?
How many shoulds are good for me daily?
What one change could I make today?
What one change could I make this month?
What one change could I make this year?
Would the change be adding something or subtracting something?
What would make me most complete?
What are my various parts?
Which deserves more attention?
Which deserves less attention?
I will declare success when . . .
Who needs to be at my renewing ceremony?
What kind of water will I use?

Once you have done this diagnosis, you might decide to share it with someone else. You are well on your way to getting your timing belt changed—not fixed, but changed. It will wear out again if you are lucky enough to live long.

When someone asks you why you seem so different, just say you got lucky. You were in the right place at the right time. Mammon picked you up out of the water where God put you. Then God picked you up out of the water where Mammon orphaned you. And the cycle went on and on.

Selected References

Alexander, Michelle. *The New Jim Crow: Mass Incarceration in the Age of Colorblindness.* New York: New Press, 2012.

BBC News. "Archbishop Justin Welby Hopes for Fixed Easter Date." January 15, 2016. http://www.bbc.com/news/uk-35326237.

Carson, Rachel. *Silent Spring.* 50th anniversary ed. Boston: Mariner Books, 2012.

Charney, Noah. "A Fake of Art." *Aeon*, February 5, 2016. https://aeon.co/essays/is-there-a-place-for-fakery-in-art-galleries-and-museums.

———. *The Art of Forgery: The Minds, Motives, and Methods of the Master Forgers.* London: Phaidon, 2015.

Chun, Wendy Hui Kyong. *Updating to Remain the Same: Habitual New Media.* Cambridge, MA: MIT Press, 2016.

Cone, James H. *God of the Oppressed.* Rev. ed. Maryknoll, NY: Orbis, 2000.

Fischer, Norman. *Opening to You: Zen-Inspired Translations of the Psalms.* New York: Penguin Compass, 2003.

"Gaslighting." EQI.org, http://eqi.org/gaslighting.htm.

Gawandi, Atul. *Being Mortal.* Toronto: Anchor Canada, 2017.

Harris-Gershon, David. "The Origin of 'Scapegoat,' Donald Trump & Ta-Nehisi Coates: A Thought for Progressives on Yom Kippur." *Tikkun Daily*, September 23, 2015. http://www.tikkun.org/tikkundaily/2015/09/23/the-origin-of-scapegoat-donald-trump-ta-nehisi-coates-a-thought-for-progressives-on-yom-kippur.

Heffernan, Virginia. *Magic and Loss: The Internet as Art.* New York: Simon and Schuster, 2016.

Hoagland, Edward. "A Country for Old Men." *American Scholar*, winter 2009.

———. "Heaven and Nature." *Harper's*, March 1988.

———. *On Nature: Selected Essays.* Guilford, CT: Lyons Press, 2003.

———. "Knights and Squires: For the Love of the Tugs." *Village Voice*, May 29, 1969.

———. "The Problem of the Golden Rule." *Commentary*, August 1969.

———. *Sex and the River Styx.* White River Junction, VT: Chelsea Green Publishing, 2011.

Howard, Philip. *Pax Technica: How the Internet of Things May Set Us Free or Lock Us Up.* New Haven, CT: Yale University Press, 2015.

"The Keeper." *New Yorker*, n.d. https://www.newyorker.com/goings-on-about-town/art/the-keeper.

Kincaid, Jamaica. *Lucy.* New York: Twayne, 1994.

Kondo, Marie. *The Life-Changing Magic of Tidying Up: The Japanese Art of Decluttering and Organizing.* Berkeley, CA: Ten Speed Press, 2014.

Kott, Ruth. "Mortal Thoughts." *University of Chicago Magazine*, winter 2016. https://mag. uchicago.edu/science-medicine/mortal-thoughts.

Kübler-Ross, Elisabeth. *The Wheel of Life: A Memoir of Living and Dying*. 1997; New York: Scribner, 2014.

Mendelson, Edward. "In the Depths of the Digital Age." *New York Review of Books*, June 23, 2016. http://www.nybooks.com/articles/2016/06/23/depths-of-the-digital-age.

Myers, Ched. "Everything Will Live Where the River Goes." *Sojourners*, April 2012. https:// soho.net/magazine/april-2012/everything-will-live-where-river-goes.

Philips, Adam. *Missing Out: In Praise of the Unlived Life*. New York: Picador/Farrar, Strauss and Giroux, 2014.

Pope Francis. "Encyclical Letter Laudato Si' of the Holy Father Francis on Care for Our Common Home." http://w2.vatican.va/content/francesco/en/encyclicals/documents/papa-francesco_20150524_enciclica-laudato-si.html.

Pritchard, Evan. *No Word for Time: The Way of the Algonquin People*. San Francisco: Council Oak Books, 2001.

Pynchon, Thomas. *Gravity's Rainbow*. 1972; New York: Penguin, 2006.

Schade, Leah. *Creation-Crisis Preaching: Ecology, Theology, and the Pulpit*. St. Louis: Chalice Press, 2015.

Schaper, Donna. *Prayers for People Who Say They Can't Pray*. Nashville: Abingdon Press, 2014.

Schor, Juliet. *The Overworked American: The Unexpected Decline of Leisure*. New York: Basic Books, 2000.

Schulz, Kathryn. *Being Wrong: Adventures in the Margin of Error*. New York: HarperCollins, 2011.

Sober, Elliot. *Ockham's Razors: A User's Manual*. Cambridge: Cambridge University Press, 2015.

———. "Why Is Simpler Better?" *Aeon*, May 3, 2016. https://aeon.co/essays/are-scientific-theories-really-better-when-they-are-simpler.

Taylor, Mark C. *Speed Limits: Where Time Went and Why We Have So Little Left*. New Haven, CT: Yale University Press, 2014.

Thompson, Erin. "Why People Collect Art." *Aeon*, August 23, 2016. https://aeon.co/essays/what-drives-art-collectors-to-buy-and-display-their-finds.

Thorngate, Steve. "Holy Water Everywhere: Baptism and Place." *Christian Century*, December 10, 2014. https://www.christiancentury.org/article/2014-12/holy-water-everywhere.

Wajcman, Judy. *Pressed for Time: The Acceleration of Life in Digital Capitalism*. Chicago: University of Chicago Press, 2016.

Warren, LaShawn. "A Christian in Public and Private." *Reflections: A Magazine of Theological and Ethical Inquiry from Yale Divinity School*, 2016. http://reflections.yale.edu/article/all-together-now-pluralism-and-faith/christian-public-and-private.

Waskow, Arthur. "Rainbow Sign: A Jewish Approach to the Danger of Global Eco-Disaster." *Jewcology*, August 9, 2010, http://jewcology.org/resources/rainbow-sign-a-Jewish-approach-to-the-danger-of-global-eco-disaster.

Weisman, Alan. *The World without Us*. Toronto: HarperCollins Canada, 2010.

Woletz, Bob. "JZ Holden and Jules Feiffer: Humor and Truth Spark Outrage, then a Union." *New York Times*, September 18, 2016. https://www.nytimes.com/2016/09/18/fashion/weddings/jz-holden-and-jules-feiffer-married.html.

Zahn, Max. "Zen and the Art of Zombie Killing: A Buddhist Anti-Tech Manifesto." *Religion Dispatches*, April 7, 2016. http://religiondispatches.org/zen-and-the-art-of-zombie-killing-a-buddhist-anti-tech-manifesto.

The *New York Times* articles referenced in chapter 11 are:

Castle, Stephen. "London Elects Muslim Mayor in Tense Race." *New York Times*, May 7, 2016. https://www.nytimes.com/2016/05/07/world/europe/britain-election-results.html.

Davey, Monica, and Giovanni Russonello. "Chicago Survey Finds Many See City Gone Awry," *New York Times*, May 6, 2016. https://www.nytimes.com/2016/05/07/us/chicago-racial-divisions-survey.html.

Onishi, Norimitsu, and Hopewell Chin'ono. "Mugabe's Frailty Shows, and Power Grab Brews." *New York Times*, May 8, 2016. https://www.nytimes.com/2016/05/08/world/africa/zimbabwe-president-robert-mugabe-falters.html.

Philipps, Dave. "One Photo, 16 Clenched Fists and a Glimpse of a Riven West Point." *New York Times*, May 7, 2016. https://www.nytimes.com/2016/05/07/us/raised-fist-photo-by-black-women-at-west-point-spurs-inquiry.html.

Index